ISSUE 20, FEBRUARY 2024

# AUSTRALIAN FOREIGN AFFAIRS

# Contributors

**Elizabeth Buchanan** is a project director at West Point Military Academy and an associate of the National Security College at the Australian National University.

**Jack Corbett** is head of the School of Social Sciences at Monash University and co-director of the Resilient and Sustainable Islands Initiative.

**Andrew Davies** has researched, written about and lectured on defence policy at the Department of Defence, the Australian Strategic Policy Institute and the Australian National University.

**Hervé Lemahieu** is director of research at the Lowy Institute and a consulting senior fellow at the Lee Kuan Yew School of Public Policy.

**Paul Monk** is the former head of the China desk in the Defence Intelligence Organisation.

**Susannah Patton** is director of the South-East Asia program at the Lowy Institute. She previously worked as a senior analyst in the Office of National Intelligence.

**Hugh White** is an emeritus professor of strategic studies at the Australian National University.

Australian Foreign Affairs is published three times a year by Australian Foreign Affairs Pty Ltd. Publisher: Morry Schwartz. Editor-in-chief: Erik Jensen. ISBN 978-1-76064-4314 ISSN 2208-5912  Subscriptions – 1 year print & digital auto-renew (3 issues): $49.99 within Australia incl. GST. 1 year print and digital subscription (3 issues): $59.99 within Australia incl. GST. 2 year print & digital (6 issues): $114.99 within Australia incl. GST. 1 year digital only auto-renew: $29.99. Payment may be made by MasterCard, Visa or Amex, or by cheque made out to Schwartz Books Pty Ltd. Payment includes postage and handling. To subscribe, fill out the form inside this issue, subscribe online at www.australianforeignaffairs.com, email subscribe@australianforeignaffairs.com or phone 1800 077 514 / 61 3 9486 0288. Correspondence should be addressed to: The Editor, Australian Foreign Affairs, 22–24 Northumberland Street, Collingwood, VIC, 3066 Australia Phone: 61 3 9486 0288 / Fax: 61 3 9486 0244 Email: enquiries@australianforeignaffairs.com. Editor: Jonathan Pearlman. Deputy Editor: Rebecca Bauert. Associate Editor: Chris Feik. Publicity: Anna Lensky. Design: Peter Long. Production Coordination: Marilyn de Castro. Typesetting: Tristan Main. Cover photograph: Leon Neal / PA Images / Alamy. Printed in Australia by McPherson's Printing Group.

## Editor's Note

# DEAD IN THE WATER

The late Allan Gyngell, one of Australia's leading foreign policy advisers and thinkers, was no quietist or fence-sitter, but he was reluctant to pass judgement on AUKUS.

Gyngell's inconclusiveness on AUKUS was a consequence of his piercing criticism of it: that the Morrison and Albanese governments had betrayed the nation by never explaining their plan to acquire nuclear-powered submarines. This disgraceful public failing prompted him, to his regret, to reserve judgement on the plan's merits.

"The most surprising thing about this announcement of the largest project ever undertaken by the Commonwealth of Australia remains the fact that there has been no formal articulation of the reasons for the decision," he told the *Australia in the World* podcast in March 2023. "No report, no speech to parliament, no speech at all, other than the sales patter from successive governments: 'China is more assertive, the rules-based order is under threat, nuclear submarines are just what Australia needs.'"

Gyngell's criticism has proven increasingly urgent. Part of the reason for Canberra's AUKUS silence was that former prime minister

Scott Morrison, on the eve of AUKUS being unveiled, gave Anthony Albanese only hours to consider Labor's position – and Albanese, aware of the political implications of saying no or of prevaricating, duly fell in behind it. So there has been no political debate about this $368-billion decision on which the nation's future security depends.

But the silence in Canberra makes it even more necessary to debate AUKUS. And, when scrutinised, serious questions emerge about its risks, benefits, costs and logistics.

Some of these questions involve the "patter", as Gyngell put it. The government says the capabilities provided by nuclear-powered submarines – their stealth, speed and range – will help to deter China. This simple claim – that a better boat must make Australia more secure – has made AUKUS an easy political sell. But, like much about AUKUS, the appeal starts to fade as the assertion is tested. What alternative capabilities, for instance, could $368 billion (or less) buy? Does Australia need to operate so far from shore? How much does this so-called sovereign capability depend on Australia's partners?

Questions also arise about how this defence capability matches Australia's broader strategic and foreign policy goals. When the AUKUS pact was unveiled in September 2021, little attempt was made to brief Australia's regional neighbours. This oversight was rectified when Australia announced the submarine project's "optimal pathway" in March 2023, which involved extensive foreign briefings. And yet the region's responses to AUKUS have often been misunderstood, though they reveal stark differences between Australia and its neighbours on how to handle rising tensions in Asia.

Perhaps most significant are the serious questions about whether AUKUS will ever be delivered at all. It is the most expensive – and arguably the most ambitious – defence acquisition in Australian history. But details about AUKUS's logistics have quickly dimmed its glow. The hurdles ahead keep mounting: technical challenges, skills and workforce issues, the uncertainties of US politics.

In the end, debate about the strategic merits of nuclear-powered submarines may prove irrelevant: the plan may be impossible. If, as Hugh White says, AUKUS is a charade, it needs to be abandoned quickly – to lower the wasted costs, and to reduce the growing risk that Australia will be left defenceless.

*Jonathan Pearlman*

# FATAL SHORES

## AUKUS is a grave mistake

Hugh White

AUKUS is something of a phenomenon. The bombshell announcement at 7 a.m. on 15 September 2021 must rank as one of the most spectacular policy coups in Australia's history. Though details were scarce, it was immediately and almost universally acclaimed as a triumph. Since then, state governments, industries, universities and many other sectors and institutions have scrambled to seize its apparently limitless opportunities. Internationally, too, it has been a sensation, seen as transforming the Asian strategic balance and reshaping the global order. All this has given AUKUS an aura of inevitability. It feels too big and too bold to fail.

Yet doubts are growing. The more we learn about AUKUS, the more pressing the questions about it become. There are some obvious concerns about the astonishing cost, the environmental risks and the nuclear proliferation consequences. And there are more fundamental questions about whether we need nuclear-powered submarines at all, whether the plan to get them could possibly work, and whether the wider strategic consequences will make us less rather than more secure. I think these issues will overwhelm AUKUS and sink it. The sooner that happens the better, because until AUKUS is abandoned we will not be able to get defence policy back on track and start responding effectively to the extraordinary strategic challenges that Australia faces today. And to do that we have to understand why AUKUS is such a debacle, and how it happened.

## What is AUKUS?

First, we must sort out what AUKUS really is. It is spoken of as a radical transformation of Australia's strategic posture based on a completely new level of strategic engagement between America, Britain and Australia, involving not just the plan for Australia to get nuclear-powered submarines but much more besides. There is also the so-called "Second Pillar" of AUKUS, which promises closer-than-ever research cooperation into the military applications of new technologies, the integration of the three partners' defence industries, and plans for rotational deployments of American and British submarines to Australian ports. Underlying all this is a reassuring assumption that America and Britain have deepened and strengthened their commitments to Australia's defence. Thanks to AUKUS, we feel less alone.

But most of this is window-dressing at best. Enthusiasts often suggest that the Second Pillar of deepening cooperation on advanced capabilities – such as AI, advanced cyber, hypersonics and autonomous vehicles – is the most important part of AUKUS. It is supposed to "develop and provide joint advanced military capabilities to promote security and stability in the Indo-Pacific region". Scepticism is in order. It is easy to talk up the military potential of exotic new technologies, but delivering real capability is a different matter. It is, moreover, unlikely that AUKUS will help Australia gain better access to any important new developments that materialise. Our contribution will be too modest to entice Washington or London to more generously share the strategically and commercially sensitive crown jewels of their research in these areas than would have happened anyway.

There is even less substance to the claim that AUKUS will integrate our defence industry with America's and Britain's, opening immense new opportunities for Australian companies and workers. It is naive to expect that the easing of some legislative constraints on Australian participation in US defence procurement will send a flood of work our way. In the highly politicised world of defence contracting, our AUKUS partners will always bend over backwards to keep this work at home. No strategic or commercial imperatives will compel them to send it our way. Defence industry integration is more likely to mean that work on Australian projects will flow to America and Britain than the other way round. It will also limit our scope for cooperation with other partners.

Nor is there much substance to the proposal to rotationally deploy US and UK submarines through our ports. This plan is likely to be curtailed or dropped because both the US and the UK navies are struggling to meet their existing tasks. The last thing they need is an additional drain on their fleet availability. The deployments that do take place will have little or no impact on the military balance in Asia or on Australia's security. Too few UK boats will be sent here to shift the needle one way or the other. And basing US subs near Perth makes scant difference to US submarine operations against China: they would be almost as close to China if they stayed in Hawaii.

Above all, it is an illusion to think that AUKUS strengthens America's or Britain's guarantee of our security. In Britain's case, there is nothing to strengthen, because it has no commitment to our defence. After fraying for decades, the last link of the old imperial defence bond was unceremoniously severed over fifty years ago when Britain finally pulled out of Asia and withdrew East of Suez. No defence treaty has taken its place, and nothing in AUKUS changes that. Nor does AUKUS enhance the formal commitments between America and Australia under ANZUS, or materially alter the underlying balance of interests which will determine whether – and, if so, how far – America would come to our aid in a crisis. All AUKUS does is further entangle Australia in US policy in Asia, which is not at all the same thing. We will come back to this later.

**No government had seriously considered nuclear propulsion for our new subs before AUKUS**

That leaves the plan for nuclear-powered submarines as the real substance of AUKUS, and the whole idea will stand or fall on the success or failure of that plan. And that will depend on the answers to two basic questions: does Australia need nuclear-powered submarines, and will the AUKUS plan deliver them?

## Does Australia need nuclear-powered submarines?

It is a simple but vital question that too few people have thought to ask either before the agreement was announced or since. The argument for having submarines of some kind is pretty clear. Our strategic setting is fundamentally maritime. As ships become more vulnerable to detection and attack, we have increasingly relied on submarines as the best way to conduct maritime operations beyond the range of land-based air power. That is why successive governments have agreed that replacing our fleet of six Collins-class submarines is a high priority. But why do we need nuclear-powered subs? No government had seriously considered nuclear propulsion for our new subs before the AUKUS plan was hatched. Indeed, governments had always dismissed the idea whenever amateur enthusiasts argued for it. Instead, Canberra was fully committed to conventional submarines and had embarked on an ambitious and extremely expensive project to build twelve Attack-class vessels to a French design. So why did they dump that project and opt for nuclear-powered instead? And do those reasons hold water?

Something about the idea of nuclear power captures many people's imaginations. They are convinced that nuclear-powered submarines are in a class of their own and are so obviously far superior to conventionally powered boats that no further analysis is necessary. Enthusiasts call them the "apex predator" of the seas, and suggest that even a handful of them can fundamentally change the maritime strategic balance in our region. But this is not true. A nuclear-powered submarine of the kind we are supposed to be getting under AUKUS – an attack submarine, not one carrying nuclear-armed ballistic missiles – carries the same kinds of sensors and weapons as a conventionally armed sub and does the same job. Why, then, are nuclear-powered submarines supposed to be a better choice for Australia?

Like most defence investment decisions, this is basically a question of cost-effectiveness. Is the extra cost and risk of a more sophisticated piece of equipment justified by better performance in battle? The usual and instinctive response, perhaps understandably, is that the more expensive and sophisticated option must be the better choice, but long experience shows that this is seldom correct. That is because simpler and cheaper alternatives are easier to build, easier to operate, more reliable and – crucially – can be had in bigger numbers. Military history is full of cases where larger numbers of cheaper, simpler weapons systems have outperformed smaller numbers of more expensive, sophisticated adversaries. A classic example comes from the Eastern Front of World War II. The Soviets built 80,000 simple but effective T-34 tanks, which prevailed over 8000 much more advanced German Panzer IVs. As Stalin supposedly said: "Quantity has a quality all its own."

So the first key question to ask about AUKUS is whether, in Australia's circumstances, the operational advantages of nuclear-powered submarines justify the higher price tag and greater risks of buying and operating them. Before AUKUS, the answer had always been "no" – for very good reasons. For a start, the cost difference is immense. All submarine projects are expensive, but nuclear-powered submarines are *much* more expensive to build and operate than conventionally powered ones. Government cost estimates for the twelve Attack-class conventional subs were muddled or deliberately obfuscated, but the upper figure was around $100 billion – a figure so high that it must have included the costs of maintaining them over their service lives. The government has estimated that the through-life cost of the eight nuclear-powered subs planned under AUKUS will be as much as $368 billion. That is unlikely to be an underestimate. On these numbers, each nuclear-powered sub would cost five and a half times more than a French-designed conventional boat. They are also substantially more complex and riskier to build and operate. No government had previously thought that, for our needs, the benefits of nuclear propulsion would justify these far higher costs and risks.

Why, then, does the present government – like its predecessor – think differently? The main reason it has given is detectability. This is a critical issue, because a submarine's ability to avoid detection while submerged is its decisive advantage in battle. In justifying AUKUS, the government has said that over the next few decades, new detection technologies will make conventionally powered submarines much easier to detect than nuclear-powered boats – so much so that conventional subs will no longer be operationally viable. Is this right?

The government's stated concerns about detectability focus on the subs' need to regularly come up to periscope depth, close to the surface, and run their diesel engines in order to charge the batteries which power them when submerged. To do this they must raise their diesels' air intake and exhaust above the waves. The resulting "indiscretion" is not very big – the "masts" that poke into the air are just a few centimetres in diameter and a metre or so high – but it offers detection opportunities to an alert and capable enemy. "Snorting", as this procedure is known, has always been a vulnerability of conventional submarines, and a significant disadvantage compared to nuclear-powered ones. The government now claims that new detection technologies are going to make snorting submarines much more vulnerable to detection, to the point that conventionally powered submarines will become operationally ineffective against capable adversaries.

**There is no evidence that conventional boats will be more vulnerable to emerging detection technologies**

Why has the government reached this conclusion? It obviously did not think this was a big problem when it signed the French contract for twelve conventional submarines in 2016. Right up to the AUKUS announcement in 2021, it repeatedly assured us that the Attack-class was exactly the submarine we needed. In fact, the Abbott government was evidently quite relaxed about the risks of snorting when it set the requirements for these new submarines in 2015. Surprisingly, it ruled out two technologies that would have reduced the need to snort. One was the use of new-technology batteries in place of the old lead-acid types, and the other was the fitting of an air-independent propulsion system. Both innovations cut the need to snort and are becoming standard on modern conventional submarines. The government would hardly have excluded them from consideration for our conventional submarines if they believed that snorting was becoming such a critical vulnerability.

So, did the government suddenly learn, sometime between 2016 and 2021, of a dramatic and unexpected technological breakthrough in the detection of snorting conventional submarines? If so, it has not told us about it. No doubt the details would be classified, but it is odd that other well-informed governments haven't got the same message and drawn the same conclusion. Many countries with long histories of serious investment in submarines – Japan, Germany, Sweden, Italy, Spain, the Netherlands, India, Russia and, yes, China – are still building conventional submarines. If they know what our government claims to know, why aren't they also dumping these projects?

These questions become even more acute when we look at what is really happening in the arcane world of submarine detection. There is a growing consensus that the long-running high-tech cat-and-mouse contest between ever-stealthier submarine designs and increasingly sensitive detection systems is now taking a decisive turn in the submarine hunters' favour. A whole range of technologies seem poised to make submarines easier to find. They include not just refinements in well-established acoustic and magnetic methods, but new approaches including the detection of disturbances in the ocean from a submarine's displacement and wake and from minute chemical traces left by submarines as they pass through the water, using data collected by satellites and uncrewed underwater drones. These trends were surveyed and assessed in a compelling report published in May 2020 by the government-funded National Security College. It concluded that "the oceans are, in most circumstances, at least likely and, from some perspectives, very likely to become transparent by the 2050s", which means that for submarines "the coming counter-detection task may be insuperable".

What makes this conclusion really significant for AUKUS is that the report focused specifically on nuclear-powered submarines. It showed that the big trends in submarine detection are raising doubts about the future stealth of nuclear-powered boats that are just as grave as – or even graver than – those about conventional subs. That is not surprising, because although they do not need to snort, nuclear boats are bigger, faster, hotter and, in some circumstances, noisier than conventionally powered subs, all of which makes them inherently easier to find. Nor is it surprising that cutting-edge submarine-detection research, which is mostly funded by the big nuclear-armed powers, focuses on finding nuclear-powered subs. Their highest priority is finding their adversaries' nuclear-powered, nuclear-armed ballistic-missile submarines (SSBNs).

All this raises real questions about whether we should be investing in any kind of crewed submarines – conventional or nuclear. But it also seriously undermines the government's argument for abandoning conventional submarines in favour of nuclear-powered ones, because there is no evidence that conventional boats will be more vulnerable to emerging detection technologies than nuclear subs. If that claim is the primary basis for our decision to go nuclear, then the government has a lot more explaining to do.

But what about the other arguments for nuclear-powered subs? Their biggest advantage is speed. Conventional submarines must go slowly when submerged because the faster they go, the quicker their batteries discharge, and the more often they have to snort. Nuclear boats have power to spare and can sustain speeds two or three times faster than a conventional boat. Conventional subs are too slow to chase targets, so they must lie in wait for their targets to come to them, whereas nuclear subs can hunt their prey more proactively. And in some circumstances, nuclear submarines can use their speed to evade detection in ways that conventional boats cannot. But the most important advantage in Australia's situation is what it means for transit times between our submarine bases and distant areas of operations.

This is a big plus. A nuclear submarine can deploy to a distant area of operations much faster than a conventional boat, so it can spend a bigger proportion of its mission actually hunting the adversary. What that means has been explained by the Minster for Defence Industry, Pat Conroy:

> A diesel-powered submarine might spend about half of its time on an operation in transit. By contrast, for the same operation a nuclear-powered submarine would spend 15 to 20 per cent of its time in transit. In this example, let's say a theoretical 70-day operation, a diesel-electric submarine would spend 35 days in transit and 35 days on station. Meanwhile, a nuclear-powered submarine would spend just 15 days in transit and 55 days on station. For Australia's circumstances, where transit distances are necessarily long, this type of advantage is particularly significant. This advantage is compounded by the fact that nuclear-powered submarines can generally patrol longer. This means that a nuclear-powered submarine can be seen as the equivalent of two diesel-electric submarines in terms of patrol coverage.

But this advantage must be set against the difference in cost, and what that means for fleet size. A nuclear-powered submarine might be the equivalent of two conventional boats, but they cost over five times as much. For the $368 billion we are planning to spend on eight AUKUS boats, we could have a fleet of more than forty conventional submarines. This huge difference in numbers swamps the advantage of nuclear propulsion. For the same investment, a fleet of forty conventional subs would deliver more than three times as many submarines to the operational area as an eight-boat nuclear fleet. Having so many additional subs in the battle more than makes up for the advantages that each nuclear sub has over a conventional one. Alternatively, a much smaller investment – say, in a fleet of twenty-four conventional subs, costing $200 billion – would still deliver more combat power where it counts than eight nuclear-powered boats, and deliver it much faster and with far less risk of failure. Australia could easily crew this many submarines given good management and adequate pay.

One might ask, in view of these numbers, why any countries bother with nuclear-powered submarines. The answer is that for some missions that are critical to major nuclear-armed powers, a conventional submarine cannot match a nuclear boat. The most important of these is hunting an adversary's nuclear-powered subs, especially their nuclear-armed ballistic-missile submarines. Another is escorting their aircraft carrier battle groups. These missions require the speed that only nuclear propulsion can provide, and if these are the missions that a submarine force is designed to undertake, then the cost of nuclear propulsion is probably justified.

Are these priority missions for Australia's submarine force? That depends on what our armed forces should be designed primarily to do. Are we building our forces to defend ourselves and our close neighbours, or to fight alongside America against China? This is the contemporary form of the oldest debate in Australian defence policy – the debate between depending on our allies or defending ourselves – but the choice has become both starker and more urgent as strategic risks in Asia have grown with the escalating rivalry between America and China. Whichever choice we make, it is clear that we will need to spend a lot more on our armed forces than we have for many decades, but to spend that money effectively we must decide what we want our forces to do in the new and unprecedented strategic circumstances we face. Do we want to help America defeat China in a full-scale war to preserve its leadership in Asia, or do we aim to defend ourselves against a major power like China (or perhaps, one day, India) in an Asia which America no longer dominates? Unfortunately, the Albanese government's 2023 Defence Strategic Review leaned both ways at once. Some passages seemed to return to the old "Defence of Australia" policy, while others prioritised supporting America in a major war against China.

**The defence of seaborne trade is no longer operationally feasible**

This muddle no doubt reflects any government's instinctive preference to avoid a difficult decision by trying to do two things at once. But that will not work, because the two alternative strategies call for very different kinds of forces, and we certainly cannot afford to do both. So either we design our capabilities to help America project power against China, or we design them to prevent China projecting power against us. The choice between nuclear-powered and conventional submarines sits at the crux of this divide, and shows how sharply these differing conceptions of our strategic priorities pull our force plans in opposite directions. If the primary task of our submarine fleet is to team up with the US Navy to hunt Chinese ballistic-missile subs or escort US carriers in the South China

Sea, then nuclear propulsion *might* make operational sense. If, on the other hand, our primary military task is to prevent China projecting power by sea against us or our close neighbours, then nuclear-powered submarines make no operational sense at all.

Because the government is so muddled about Australia's primary strategic objective, it has never been able to offer a crisp, clear and credible explanation of the specific operational tasks our submarines are supposed to fulfil. It has not come out boldly and acknowledged that they are intended for the kind of operations which would genuinely require nuclear propulsion, like hunting Chinese SSBNs. Instead, it has suggested that their primary role will be protecting Australia's seaborne trade routes. In the government's most detailed attempt to explain publicly the operational purpose of nuclear-powered submarines for Australia, the defence department's Head of Nuclear-Powered Submarine Capability focused specifically and almost exclusively on this function. He said that the key rationale for nuclear submarines was:

> the need for Australia to be able to preserve, as a matter of economic survival, the integrity of our vital and extensive sea lines of communication. The SSN [nuclear-powered submarine] will not only play a critical part in the preservation of these arteries, but is uniquely placed in many respects to consistently deny or deter an adversary from choking these arteries off, especially those more distant from our island continent.

Ministers have made the same argument. Pat Conroy, for example, has said we need nuclear-powered submarines "to patrol and protect sea trade routes far from home". But as a justification for a fleet of nuclear-powered submarines, this makes no sense at all. Partly it is just a question of numbers: in recent years there were over 17,000 voyages to Australian ports from overseas. A fleet of eight submarines, of which no more than four might be at sea at a time, could offer protection to only the tiniest fraction of that number. But it also flows from the nature of submarine operations. Submarines are very effective for attacking ships, but they are not at all suited to defending them. That requires capabilities that can defeat the full range of threats to shipping – not just subsurface and surface but airborne threats too, which submarines cannot touch, not to mention sea mines. The broader reality is that long-term technological trends, which have made ships of all kinds easier to find and hit – and thus much harder to defend – means the defence of seaborne trade is no longer operationally feasible. The only credible approach is to deter attacks on our trade by threatening to attack an adversary's, and for that a larger fleet of conventional subs would generally be more cost-effective than a smaller fleet of nuclear boats.

Other AUKUS advocates have suggested different operational priorities to justify nuclear-powered submarines. It has been claimed, for example, that a fleet of nuclear-powered subs would enable us for the first time to launch missile strikes on targets in China itself. This would supposedly help defend Australia by providing a decisive deterrent to Chinese aggression. But there are two flaws in this argument. First, this is not something that only nuclear-powered subs can do; conventionally powered submarines are equally capable of launching land-strike missiles, and a larger fleet of conventional boats could arguably deliver more missile strikes than a small fleet of nuclear boats. Second, and more importantly, striking targets on Chinese territory is unlikely to be a winning strategy for Australia in a war with China. The biggest strike campaign we could launch would make little impact on China, except to strengthen its resolve against us, and China's capacity to hit us is far, far greater than our capacity to hit them. Lacking what Cold War strategists called "escalation dominance", Canberra would find that threatening targets in China would be more likely to provoke than deter Beijing.

All these suggested roles for Australian nuclear-powered subs overlook what is undoubtedly the primary role for any Australian submarine force in the years ahead. We face an era in which Asia's great powers are stronger and more ambitious than ever before, and America's strategic role in Asia, and its ability and willingness to defend Australia, is more uncertain than ever before. We consequently face a higher risk than ever before of having to confront a military threat from an Asian great power without the support of a major ally. In these circumstances, as the government itself suggests in parts of its Defence Strategic Review, the primary role of our defence force is to deny our air and sea approaches to hostile forces. In that case, the primary role of our submarines is to operate, independently of our allies, to interdict hostile naval forces projecting power towards Australia and its close neighbours.

To do this we need submarines deployed in many of the sea passages through the archipelago across our north, where opportunities for attack are best. For this task, a bigger fleet of conventional boats would be much more effective than the AUKUS nuclear option. Above all it is a question of numbers. Blocking the archipelago requires a lot of submarines – as many as six or eight on station at any one time, which means a total fleet of at least twenty-four boats. A fleet of nuclear-powered submarines that big is simply not possible, and conventional boats can fulfil this role perfectly well. They can also perform other important duties, including strike operations against an adversary's forward-operating bases established in our northern approaches. In all these highest-priority operations, a bigger fleet of conventional boats offers more subs carrying more weapons in more places more of the time – for less money and with less risk.

**That "optimal pathway" has turned out to be even longer and more complex than expected**

It is striking that at no point since AUKUS was first announced has a prime minster or a defence minster given a substantial, detailed statement of the strategic rationale of the biggest defence capability commitment Australia has ever made. The lack of a clear military strategy has made it all too easy to fudge the critical questions of what our forces are supposed to do, and whether we need nuclear-powered submarines to do it. And later, when we explore the wider strategic setting of AUKUS, it will become clear why building our forces to support America is the wrong choice, and that nuclear-powered submarines are therefore not what we need.

## Will the AUKUS plan work?

Before we get to that, however, we need to explore a second simple question that people have only recently begun to ask. Will AUKUS actually deliver any submarines? No one had any idea how the agreement was supposed to work when it was first announced back in September 2021. Nor did they have any idea how much the subs would cost, or how long it would take to deliver them. These "details" were all left to be worked out over the following eighteen months. They were duly announced in March 2023 when Albanese, with Joe Biden and Rishi Sunak, revealed what was boldly called the "optimal pathway" to an Australian nuclear-powered submarine capability. That pathway has turned out to be even longer and more complex than expected. The first step is a radical overhaul and upgrade of the old Collins-class boats to keep them going until the new submarines arrive. The second step happens from the early 2030s, when we get between three and five second-hand Virginia-class submarines from America. Finally, in the early 2040s, the first of eight new AUKUS-class subs, built in Australia to a British–Australian design, will enter service. The rest will follow at three-year intervals, so if all goes according to plan Australia will receive the last of eight AUKUS-class nuclear-powered subs in the mid-2060s. That is forty years from now. If the plan suffers no more than the usual kinds of delays in such projects, the eighth boat won't arrive until well into the 2070s. These timeframes are, of course, absurd in light of the government's ready acknowledgement that we face major new strategic risks right now. But the bigger problem is the high likelihood – almost a certainty, really – that the plan will collapse long before then, and probably long before the first nuclear-powered submarine enters service with the RAN. To see why, let's go through the plan step by step.

The first step is the major and very complex upgrade of the Collins-class boats, called a LOTE (life-of-type extension). Though this is the simplest part of the plan, it is in itself a daunting task. It involves a virtual rebuilding of the old Collins boats, replacing many of their key systems and components. Submarine upgrade projects like this are always plagued with unexpected problems and unplanned demands, and this one is being started far too late. It has been clear for years that a major LOTE would be necessary to avoid a gap between the Collins class and its replacement, but successive governments have unaccountably delayed serious preparations for the task. Even now the scope of the project has not been finalised, and serious work will not start until 2026. Defence has acknowledged that the project involves more than 1000 tasks for each submarine, that many of the tasks are interdependent, and that schedule overruns are virtually certain. There is now no chance that the upgrades will proceed quickly enough to prevent a major drop in the number of Collins-class subs fit to go to sea and ready to fight. That is a big problem, and not just because we will be unprepared to meet threats that arise over the next twenty-five years while the transition to nuclear-powered boats is supposed to take place. Any sustained cut in the number of subs available for operations will mean too few crew members get the training and experience they need to become competent submariners. This problem is especially serious because the Virginia-class boats have a crew of 120 – twice as many as the Collins boats. The whole AUKUS plan may well collapse because we will not have the crews to operate nuclear-powered subs if and when they begin to arrive.

Second, even if the Collins-class LOTE goes better than expected, there are real questions about whether the RAN will be prepared to take delivery of the Virginia-class submarines by the early 2030s. It has less than a decade to learn to operate, maintain and support nuclear-powered submarines, including their nuclear reactors. The challenge was made clear by the then chief of the US Navy, Admiral Gilday. Speaking of AUKUS, he said, "In America, we believe that we can do anything, but some days when I sit back and I think, boy, if we had to start a nuclear-submarine program from a cold start today, that is a big leap."

Our navy and defence organisations have never faced a challenge like this. With its dismal record of managing much simpler tasks, the chances of the RAN being ready to operate Virginia-class subs safely and effectively and on schedule when the AUKUS plan requires are very low, especially when it must simultaneously deliver the Collins-class LOTE, prepare to build the AUKUS-class boats, and complete a massive and highly problematic program of surface-warship construction. If it fails, our AUKUS partners will not step into the breach and offer their crews to operate our subs. They suffer crew shortages and maintenance problems of their own, so will have no spare capacity to get us out of trouble. And if the Virginias cannot be brought into service on time, the whole AUKUS plan collapses. We will be without a submarine capability for several dangerous decades, and the skills-base of our submarine service will die away, leaving us unable to operate the AUKUS-class boats.

But this is not the biggest threat to this phase of the AUKUS plan. There are even more serious problems in Washington. America has never sold nuclear-powered submarines to another country, and already both the US Navy and Congress have signalled real and very reasonable doubts about whether it is wise to do so now. Late last year the Australian government hailed the passage through the US Congress of legislation allowing the transfer of nuclear-propulsion technology and Virginia-class submarines. But those approvals came with explicit conditions, especially in relation to passing US submarines to Australia. Before those transfers can proceed, whoever is president at the time will have to certify not just that Australia has the capacity to operate the vessels, but also that it is consistent with US foreign policy and national security interests, that it will not degrade US undersea capabilities, and that America has made sufficient

**America has no Virginia-class submarines to spare**

submarine production and maintenance investments. None of these conditions can be taken for granted, but the last two are especially fraught because the second phase of the AUKUS plan faces a fundamental problem. America has no Virginia-class submarines to spare. These submarines are becoming more critical to US naval strategy as major surface ships become more vulnerable, while the threat from Chinese submarines grows. For years Washington's plans to expand the Virginia-class fleet have been derailed by deep systemic problems in the US submarine-building and maintenance industry. The number of boats stuck in repair yards has grown, while the building yards have consistently failed to meet their targets. Instead of delivering two new Virginia-class boats per year, the two yards that build them have only delivered 1.3 boats per year. The US Navy and members of Congress have made it clear that they will not agree to sell Virginia-class boats to Australia unless that changes. Admiral Gilday has said it could only happen if US production increased to two boats per year. Key Republican Congress members have gone further, warning that they would not approve the sale unless production reached 2.5 boats per year. There is real doubt that these targets can be met: if anything, the problems in US submarine construction are getting worse, not better, as US yards must also ramp up construction of the new Columbia-class ballistic-missile submarines at the same time. The US Congressional Budget Office (CBO), a non-partisan and highly respected research body, explored this issue in detail in an October 2023 report. Its conclusion is stark:

> It would be very difficult and expensive for the U.S submarine industry to increase production of attack submarines during a period when it must also build 1 Columbia class ship per year. (Columbia class SSBNs are two and one-half times the size of Virginia class SSNs.) Moreover, SSBNs are the Navy's highest acquisition priority. As a result, the sale of SSNs to Australia would reduce the number of attack submarines available to the Navy.

Even if these construction targets can be met, there are genuine doubts in Washington about whether it makes strategic sense for America to pass submarines to Australia rather than keeping them for the US fleet. These doubts were pungently expressed in a report in May 2023 from the US Congressional Research Service (CRS) – another non-partisan and highly respected research body:

> Skeptics of transferring Virginia-class SSNs from the United States to Australia might argue that it could weaken deterrence of potential Chinese aggression if China were to find reason to believe, correctly or not, that Australia might use the transferred Virginia-class boats less effectively than the U.S. Navy would use them if the boats were retained in U.S. Navy service, or that Australia might not involve its military, including its Virginia-class boats, in U.S.–China crises or conflicts that Australia viewed as not engaging important Australian interests. In connection with the latter scenario, Australian Defence Minister Richard Marles

> in March 2023 reportedly confirmed that in exchange for the Virginia-class boats, Australia's government made no promises to the United States that Australia would support the United States in a future conflict over Taiwan.

Similar concerns were raised in the CBO report and by more partisan observers. Renowned Republican defence guru Elbridge Colby has said it would be "crazy" for America to sell Australia Virginia-class subs when it has far too few available in case of war with China. And here is the opinion editor of the conservative *Wall Street Journal,* Paul Gigot, in November 2023 bemoaning the decline in US military power:

> The navy's attack submarines are the best deterrent we have against a Chinese invasion of Taiwan. The navy says it needs 66 hulls, yet only 31 were "operationally ready" this past fiscal year. To satisfy the navy's needs, and meet our commitments under the AUKUS accords, we would have to build an average of at least 2.3 submarines a year. We are building 1.2.

These issues are fundamental to the viability of the AUKUS plan. Minsters in Canberra express perfect confidence that Congress will eventually agree to provide Virginia-class submarines to Australia. They cite strong bipartisan Congressional support for the US–Australia alliance and for a robust response to China. They also hope that the US$3 billion which Australia is contributing to the US submarine maintenance program – as well as the still-unspecified price we will pay for the Virginia-class boats themselves – will help assuage US concerns. But this money is a drop in the bucket which will make no material difference to America's submarine shortage. The fact remains that the AUKUS plan would weaken America's submarine forces in a war with China. As the CRS report argues, even if Australia promised that its RAN Virginia-class subs would fight alongside American boats in a war with China, our inexperienced crews would not operate them as effectively as US crews. And could the US be certain of our commitment? As both the reports quoted above make clear, Canberra has refused to make that promise.

**It is hard to see how the AUKUS plan can survive this yawning gap between American expectations and Australian commitments**

Kurt Campbell, the Biden administration's key Asia policymaker and the primary US architect of AUKUS, has tried to reassure Congress that Australia's commitment can be taken for granted even without such promises. He told a gathering in Washington in June 2023 that "when submarines are provided from the United States to Australia, it's not like they're lost. They will just be deployed by the closest possible allied force." But the Albanese government is very coy about any suggestion of a prior commitment to send Australian Virginia-class subs to join American forces in a war. Ministers insist that once the submarines pass to Australia, they will be under the sovereign control of the Australian government, just like any other element of our armed forces. That may well be so, but it evades the key question. No doubt it would be Australia's decision whether to send these subs to war, but is Canberra willing to promise that it would decide to send them to join US forces in a war with China? If not, it is very unlikely that Washington will agree to pass its sorely needed submarines to Australia, and it is far from clear that any Australian government can make such a commitment. It is important to understand that joining a US–China war would plunge Australia into the biggest military conflict since World War II, and one which could easily go nuclear, with very little chance that America would win. The problems that a Labor government would have in committing to join America in such a war were made clear at the ALP National Conference in August 2023, which issued a statement in reference to AUKUS:

> Labor believes that Australia's acquisition of submarines does not involve any *ante facto* commitment to participate in, or be directed in accordance with, the military operations of any other country.

It is hard to see how the AUKUS plan can survive this yawning gap between American expectations and Australian commitments. Whether or not Canberra should make that commitment is a bigger question to which we'll return, but as things stand it is refusing to do so. Unless that changes it is almost impossible to imagine Congress agreeing to sell Virginia-class subs to Australia. And if Congress will not let us buy them, there is no way to bridge the gap between the withdrawal of the Collins-class and the arrival of the AUKUS-class.

Then there is Trump. AUKUS will be in real trouble if, as seems quite likely, he returns to the White House. It was a Biden administration initiative, which alone suggests that Trump will be tempted to trash it, and he is instinctively hostile to anything which deepens American entanglement with allies like Australia. He is sure to look askance at any plan that does an ally a favour at the expense of America. Nor will the danger pass if Trump leaves the stage, because his isolationism is now endemic in the Republican Party. Today's Republicans may be deeply hostile to China, but they are also becoming less and less interested in supporting allies at America's expense, so AUKUS would be under threat from any future Republican president. It won't necessarily be much safer under future Democrat presidents either, because their party too is nurturing its own version of the new isolationism.

But let's assume, for the sake of argument, that America agrees to sell us some Virginia-class subs and that the RAN, having successfully completed the Collins-class LOTE and sustained a sufficient pool of trained submariners, learns to operate the Virginia-class safely and effectively. Then we face the challenges of phase three of the AUKUS plan, which involves designing, building and bringing into service the AUKUS-class submarines. Britain is supposed to build the first of the class for the Royal Navy, and to iron out the early problems, before production of submarines for the RAN begins in South Australia. Both the British and the Australian ends of this cooperative program will have to deliver if the AUKUS plan is to work. It is more than likely that both will fail.

Let's start with the British. The longer-term future of Australia's submarine capability is very much in their hands. It is clear that the AUKUS-class will be a British design, optimised to meet British needs. We have now committed ourselves to buy it, even though at this stage we know almost nothing about it. We do not know how well it will perform, how hard it will be to build, how much of it can be built in Australia or how much it will cost. This is buying a pig in a poke, which is a foolish way to buy submarines or anything else. By the time these things become clear, it will be far too late to pull out without abandoning our submarine capability. We are placing complete faith in the competence and generosity of our British partners.

There are good reasons to doubt that our faith will be justified, because the UK nuclear submarine enterprise is very fragile. They have had major problems over decades in building and sustaining their submarine forces. For example, the construction of their current Astute-class attack subs has been subject to long delays and major cost overruns – almost five years late and 53 per cent over budget, according to a 2009 parliamentary report – and there have been many reported operational problems with the boats in service. Deficiencies in UK technical and workforce capacities have also had a major impact on Britain's Vanguard-class nuclear-armed ballistic-missile subs, with the refit of one of its four boats recently requiring seven years to complete.

Things are likely to get worse. The next decade or two will be especially difficult for the British nuclear submarine enterprise, as Britain tries to complete the last of the Astute-class boats, design and build the first of the new Dreadnought-class replacements for the Vanguard ballistic-missile subs, and design and build the new AUKUS-class boats to an almost impossibly tight schedule. The AUKUS plan requires the UK to deliver the first of this new class to the Royal Navy by the late 2030s which is, to put it mildly, very ambitious. The timetable will certainly slip, which will delay Australia's build program and further weaken our capability. There is a real chance of even bigger difficulties – major problems with the design, for example – that would derail the project more seriously and perhaps even lead to its collapse as other UK priorities crowd it out. Where could we turn if that happens?

**Talk of deterrence encourages the illusion that we can win wars without fighting**

And then there is Australia's end of the project. The government is committed to building our nuclear-powered submarines in Australia. This will be by far the most complex and difficult engineering project ever undertaken here. The government hopes to sidestep defence's shortcomings by entrusting the whole program to the quasi-independent Australian Submarine Agency, headed by a vice-admiral. There is no reason to think that this bit of rebadging will make any difference. Long delays and cost overruns are certain. Outright failure is a real possibility. It is hard to disagree with former Liberal foreign minister Alexander Downer's withering assessment that the plan to build the AUKUS-class boats in Adelaide is "a fairytale".

But the problems will not be over if, against all the odds, Australian-built AUKUS submarines enter service on schedule, because the RAN will then face the daunting task of operating these new submarines alongside both the remaining Collins-class and the ageing Virginia-class boat. That means the navy and its support services will, for an extended period, find itself with the extraordinarily demanding task of having to maintain three distinct training programs, three different stockholdings and logistical pipelines, three engineering and technical support teams, and three sets of operational doctrine. The problems ahead were chillingly acknowledged by Sir Nick Hine, a veteran of the British submarine enterprise. "I can say from personal experience, which has often been bitter being a nuclear submariner myself, build is hard but support is harder … It is going to be a real challenge to have a nuclear submarine capability in Australia."

The many challenges the RAN has faced, and so often failed to meet, in operating the Collins-class submarines over the past few decades shows how hard it will be to manage even one class of submarine. To manage three very different classes of submarine, two of them nuclear-powered, at the same time? It defies belief.

## How did we get here?

We find ourselves in a remarkable situation. Coalition and Labor governments have committed Australia to acquire nuclear-powered submarines that we do not need, via a plan which will almost certainly fail. The longer it takes for this to be acknowledged, the more likely it will be that our submarine capability will simply collapse as the Collins-class boats become unserviceable with no replacements in sight. This would surely count as the most disastrous defence-policy mistake in our history and one of the worst on record anywhere. How has it happened?

One problem was the decision-making process. A good process does not always produce a good decision, but a bad process almost always produces a bad one, and the process whereby Australia decided on AUKUS seems to have been very bad indeed. Reasonable standards of due diligence would require that a decision like this, given the scale and weight of the issues at stake, would only be made after extensive analysis of the strategic, operational, technical and industrial questions we have explored above. It seems none of this happened before AUKUS was announced, because too few people knew of it, and those who did had neither the time nor the expertise to undertake an analysis and offer properly informed advice. Nor perhaps did they have much inclination to raise objections to a bold idea that had already won the hearts of senior politicians. In the Robodebt era, the old traditions of frank and fearless advice are long gone.

But the question remains: why, in the absence of serious scrutiny, did the ministers and officials inside the magic circle decide to go for

AUKUS? I think there are two reasons. The first has to do with their misperception of what armed forces do. Many people, including plenty of those who make their careers in defence, find it difficult to consider clearly what the reality of war would mean for Australia. After long decades of easy peace, they are not inclined to focus on the battles we would need to fight and the forces we would need to win them. These are hard, practical questions that demand hard, practical – and often uncomfortable – answers. So instead of thinking about fighting wars, they talk about deterring them. This keeps things comfortably vague. It shifts the focus from the concrete realities of military operations and capabilities to much more nebulous questions of psychology, focusing on what might change an adversary's mind rather than what will defeat its attacks.

In this slippery realm, it is easy for optimistic assumptions to elbow aside hard analysis about the kinds of forces we need. Talk of deterrence encourages the illusion that we can win wars without fighting, that it doesn't matter much whether the forces we build can really win battles as long as they impress the adversary, and that our adversary will be impressed by our ambition rather than by forces that meet defined operational needs. Of course we do want to deter wars rather than fight them. But the force that deters best is the one that fights best, and is ready to fight soonest. So the way to maximise deterrence is to set a military strategy and quickly build forces to execute it effectively.

AUKUS is the antithesis of this. Ministers and senior officials have repeatedly claimed that Australia must have nuclear-powered submarines because they will deter adversaries better than anything else. Here, for example, is defence industry minister Pat Conroy, one of Labor's most forceful AUKUS advocates: "You deter aggression, by showing strength and putting question marks in potential aggressors' minds. And obviously, the ultimate question mark is nuclear propelled, conventionally armed attack submarines."

Why should we expect our adversaries – China, of course – to be deterred by the AUKUS plan to deploy a small fleet of nuclear-powered submarines decades from now? Does the government think that Beijing shares its view that these subs are "the ultimate question mark", the "apex predator"? It is doubtful this is the case. China understands the strengths and limits of nuclear-powered submarines. It knows that AUKUS does nothing to enhance Australia's or America's capacity to fight its forces and win, especially over the timeframes that matter to them. China is unlikely to be deterred from its ambitions by submarines that may possibly enter service decades from now. It intends its plans to mature much sooner than that.

**Washington's agenda is diplomatic and political, not military**

The second reason the magic circle of decision-makers fell for AUKUS so easily is that, for all the key players, the AUKUS submarine plan was never primarily about submarines at all. In each partner country, the submarine plan was a means to pursue other agendas and objectives. That made it easy to ignore the awkward questions that should have been asked.

Britain's agenda is easy to understand. It combines imperial nostalgia and commercial opportunism. AUKUS offers the British a chance to indulge their idea of themselves as a world power while making money at the same time. Britain still longs for something like the global role of its imperial heyday. Since Brexit they speak of a reborn "Global Britain", reaching beyond the narrow European stage to reclaim something of its old influence, especially in Asia. But this illusion confronts a stark reality. It is over fifty years since Harold Wilson formalised Britain's abandonment of its strategic mission in Asia, when he announced the withdrawal of its last military deployments East of Suez. Long before that, Britain ceased to be a significant maritime power in Asia, as we learnt to our dismay in 1942. Today, its relative weight in Asia has shrunk even further. It simply lacks the heft – economic, technological and diplomatic – to make any difference to the Asian strategic balance.

AUKUS offers a lifeline to these illusions, giving Whitehall a chance to claim a strategic role in Asia at little cost. Indeed, far from costing anything, AUKUS offers the British a splendid chance to make a profit. Boris Johnson unblushingly acknowledged this when AUKUS was unveiled in September 2021. AUKUS, he boasted, would create "hundreds of highly skilled jobs across the United Kingdom – including in Scotland, the North of England and the Midlands – taking forward this Government's driving purpose of levelling up across the whole country".

The commercial prospects for Britain are indeed enticing. It is estimated that 7000 jobs will be created by AUKUS in the UK, because even if our subs are all built in South Australia, many key components – including the reactor itself – will be made in Britain. For Johnson and his successors, the opportunity to trumpet these economic prospects looms much larger than the future of Australia's submarine force.

AUKUS is not really about submarines for America either. In purely military terms, AUKUS makes no sense for America, because at least for the next few decades it weakens the submarine forces it can deploy against China. But Washington's agenda is diplomatic and political, not military. Its aim is to lend credibility to its faltering response to China's challenge by locking in Australian support. It might surprise Australians that Washington feels the need to do that. We assume that Washington takes our support for granted. But for years US policymakers have worried that our huge trade dependency on China will encourage us to tacitly accommodate China's ambitions at America's expense, and that we would not back America in a war with China.

This worried them especially because so many other regional countries are sitting on the fence. None of the ASEAN countries has reliably taken their side. Nor has South Korea. Not even Japan, by far America's most important regional ally, is willing to promise to go to war with China over Taiwan. So Washington has been eager, even desperate, to find a regional country willing to commit. They spotted an opportunity when Canberra's relations with Beijing tanked in 2020. AUKUS offered the means to grasp it, and as a bonus to sign Britain up too. Kurt Campbell explained all this quite frankly when he described to a US audience the Biden administration's rationale for the initiative:

> The strategic significance of AUKUS is that both Australia and Great Britain have made a fundamental decision to align with us strategically, not just now [but] into the distant future.
>
> And I would say that it was not very many years ago that if you had to make an argument which countries might be prepared to reorient more closely with other countries in the region like China, Great Britain and Australia were two countries that ten years ago flirted with different kinds of orientations, and that period is changed fundamentally.

Campbell was apparently even blunter when he explained it to EU officials privately in 2022. It has been widely reported that he told them AUKUS "gets Australia off the fence and locks it in for the next 40 years". For the Biden administration, providing Australia with nuclear-powered submarines was all about cementing Australia into US strategy towards China, and committing us to go to war with China if America does. The submarines were just the bait.

And this explains Australia's motives too because, ultimately, AUKUS is not about submarines for us either. It is about strengthening Australia's strategic bond with America, which springs from a conviction that Australia's security depends on America defeating China's challenge and remaining the dominant power in Asia. So, Australia's only option is to cling more tightly to Washington than ever, and AUKUS is how we do that. This helps explain how AUKUS happened, and it also reveals how misguided it is. AUKUS is not only a flawed way to acquire new submarines, but an embodiment of the deeply flawed approach to the strategic transformation now underway in Asia, tying us more closely than ever to America's determination to remain the dominant power in Asia. That policy is doomed to fail. The massive shift of wealth and power to China since 1980 makes it impossible to perpetuate the old US-led order, and trying to do so risks a catastrophic war. Instead of trying to support America in preserving the old order, we should be doing all we can to help shape the new order that is already taking its place. And instead of supporting America's threats to go to war to defend the old order, we should be doing all we can to prevent it launching a disastrous war that it would not win. That is why it is so important that we do not commit to go to war with America against China, as Washington will insist we do under AUKUS.

**It cannot be long before unease in the Labor Party percolates upwards**

Canberra's strategic illusions are the ultimate cause of our AUKUS debacle, but politics is involved too – on both sides of the partisan divide. In the first instance, AUKUS offered the Morrison government a pretext to dump the ill-conceived and unworkable French submarine deal on which the Coalition had staked its defence credibility.

That deal committed Australia to buy subs with no enforceable undertakings on performance, price, schedule or Australian content. By 2021 it was becoming a political liability, thanks to embarrassingly protracted negotiations with the French authorities, backsliding on local industry involvement, intractable engineering problems and highly adverse reports from independent reviewers. Claiming that newly emerging strategic and technological developments impelled a shift to nuclear-powered subs provided an excuse to abandon the deal without acknowledging these problems.

AUKUS also gave Morrison a high-profile defence initiative which provided a national security focus for the 2022 election campaign, and presented a chance to wedge Labor if they opposed it. Labor dodged that bullet by fully supporting AUKUS, partly from a pathological fear of a political brawl with the Coalition on any national security issue, but also because many of the party's leaders believe as fervently in supporting America against China as the Coalition does. It is a bipartisanship built upon political opportunism and strategic complacency on both sides.

## Where to now?

Now that Labor owns AUKUS, it is proving a difficult legacy. The problems have become much clearer since the Albanese government revealed the AUKUS "optimal pathway" in May 2023 – the complexities, risks and astronomic costs, the schedule stretching past mid-century, the implications for Australia's strategic commitments, the nuclear proliferation and nuclear waste-management issues, the constraints to be imposed on scientific research. Unease and outright opposition in the ALP have grown, fanned by trenchant and characteristically colourful criticisms from Paul Keating, and creating major ructions at the party's national conference in August 2023. Albanese and his colleagues have found these critiques difficult to answer. In the end only factional arm-twisting, some highly tendentious claims about the economic benefits and that unsustainable promise that AUKUS did not commit us to war with China prevented a boilover on the conference floor. It can only be a temporary respite, as the implications of AUKUS become clearer and doubts about it grow. It cannot be long before unease in the Labor Party percolates upwards. There are already signs of concern in Cabinet. James Curran in *The Australian Financial Review*, reporting on the national conference, wrote:

> Behind the scenes, a senior Albanese government cabinet minister, speaking on the condition of anonymity, likewise voiced strong concerns about the "high risk" of the submarines. The same minister also confirmed how completely rattled the cabinet was by Keating's AUKUS critique.

Still, the Albanese government will no doubt push ahead with AUKUS until, sooner or later, one of the probable points of failure we have described brings it to a grinding halt. The crunch is perhaps most likely to come in Washington, where a number of hurdles could prove fatal to America's willingness to sell us Virginia-class subs. They include American inability to expand their submarine production, Australian unwillingness to commit to war with China, Australian inability to meet US standards for operating nuclear submarines safely, and sheer Trumpian bloody-mindedness towards allies. However it fails, we should hope the end comes soon, with less money wasted and more time to get our force planning back on the rails, but it may already be too late to save Australia's submarine capability. It is certainly too late to replace the Collins-class fleet with a new class of conventional subs built entirely in Australia. Having wasted so much time with the ill-conceived French deal and then with AUKUS, there is now only one way to bring new submarines into service before the Collins-class boats must be retired. That would be to move as quickly as possible to buy six conventionally powered subs to an existing design built overseas. The most obvious candidate would be the German Type 214, which the navy reportedly considered as an interim capability when the Attack-class project began to go off the rails. These boats would be smaller than we ideally need, and would not meet all of our requirements, but they would allow us to sustain some submarine capability. At the same time we should launch a new project to build larger, more capable conventionally powered subs in Australia, so that before the last of the overseas-built boats were delivered, locally built boats would be coming into service, laying the foundation for the continuous build program required to sustain the much larger fleet of conventional subs we will need in the decades ahead.

But a lot of things would have to fall into place for this plan to work, and it may prove impracticable. So we should also start thinking about what we might do if our submarine capability collapses. Can we do without them? I think we could, but it would require us to rethink our maritime strategy. The key role of submarines for Australia's defence is to deny our maritime approaches to hostile ships beyond the range of land-based air and missile systems. There are three things we can do to make up for the loss of our submarine capability. One is to focus on replacing the Collins-class with uncrewed submarine drones. There seems little doubt that, in the long term, drones will play a bigger and bigger role in underwater warfare as developing technologies both improve drones' performance and render crewed subs more vulnerable to detection. Our repeated failures so far to establish a viable project to replace the Collins-class might compel us to take this necessary technological leap sooner rather than later.

**We have to take seriously the responsibility for designing and building our armed forces to defend ourselves**

Another possibility would be to extend the scale and range of our land-based systems to cover the waters that would otherwise be patrolled by subs. That would mean more and longer-range aircraft and anti-ship missiles. The third is to focus our defence closer to home, relying on a shallower but denser defensive shield, with a lot more resources devoted to shorter-range aircraft and missiles. Somewhat counterintuitively, operational analysis going all the way back to World War I suggests that concentrating our defences in this way might be more cost effective than spreading resources between longer and shorter-range systems. There are good arguments in favour of all these approaches, and of course the best path might be to do a bit of each of them. And if the pessimists are right about the increasing vulnerability of crewed submarines, whether conventional or nuclear-powered, then these might in the long run be better options anyway.

But none of this will happen unless we learn the deeper lessons of the AUKUS debacle. First, we should not commit to major defence capability investments without careful analysis of the outcome we want to achieve, and the most cost-effective means of achieving it. Second, that kind of analysis is only possible when we have set clear and realistic strategic objectives for our armed forces, and have designed a military strategy to achieve it. Third, we will only get our strategic objectives right when we realistically understand our strategic circumstances. For Australia today that means recognising some uncomfortable truths which we have for too long ignored. Above all, despite what Washington says and what we would prefer, the profound shift in wealth and power in our region means that America's role is going to change, and shrink. We cannot rely on it to keep Asia stable and Australia secure the way we have for so long. That means we have to look after ourselves, which means we have to take seriously the responsibility for designing and building our armed forces to defend ourselves. It is a long time since we have done that.

For any of this to happen we will need a much better defence and foreign policy bureaucracy, able and fearlessly willing to provide clear, forceful, authoritative and well-reasoned professional advice. History will not be gentle with senior public servants and military officers who failed to recognise or explain the pitfalls of AUKUS to their ministerial masters. We have become familiar with such failures over many years now, both in defence and in the public service more broadly – multiple failed investment projects and costly failures in Iraq and Afghanistan as well as scandals like Robodebt – but the sheer scale of AUKUS puts it in a class of its own as an exemplar of bureaucratic incompetence.

The bigger problem, however, lies at the parliamentary level, and across the political spectrum. The trends that are transforming Australia's international environment and sharply increasing our strategic risks have been evident since the turn of the century, but neither major party has yet seriously grappled with their implications for our foreign and defence policies. For a quarter of a century, as China's power and ambition grew while America faltered, both sides of politics have been content to assume that nothing is really changing. While both major parties have talked a lot about escalating strategic risks, neither side has taken any serious steps to adapt our defence and foreign polices to the new demands we face. They must recognise and accept that the historic shift in the distribution of wealth and power in Asia means an equally fundamental shift in the regional order. They can no longer assume that Asia will be managed and made safe for us by the dominant power of our former great and powerful friends, and current AUKUS partners, Britain and America. So they must devote all their diplomatic energies not to trying to preserve the old order, but to doing whatever they can to shape the new regional order that is emerging as US power fades. And they must focus their defence efforts on building forces that can protect us independently in a region which is no longer dominated by our mates, but by Asian great powers.

Instead of doing all this, our political leaders have given us the charade of AUKUS, which will stand as a fitting symbol of our failure, as a country, to respond effectively to the biggest shift in our strategic circumstances since 1788. If we are to recover from this blunder, and do better, we must start by understanding and accepting how much our region, and the world beyond it, is changing. ■

# WIDENING THE GAP

## How South-East Asia views AUKUS

Susannah Patton

In her first speech to a South-East Asian audience as foreign minister, Penny Wong reiterated Paul Keating's famous line: "Australia must find its security in Asia, not from Asia." Restating this phrase early in her new role was a signal that although the Albanese government remained committed to AUKUS and deeper ties with the United States, it would seek engagement with South-East Asia in line with a Labor tradition traceable to the Whitlam, Hawke and Keating governments. In so doing, it would tread a different path from the Morrison government, which never really sustained a high-level focus on this region.

To reconcile Australia's alliance relations with regional engagement, Wong has articulated a concept of "strategic equilibrium". Wong has proposed that a balance of power, with no single country dominating, will provide an environment in which South-East Asian countries can "make their own sovereign choices, including about their alignments and partnerships". This concept is a neat way of framing Australia's investment in AUKUS and other defence acquisitions as contributions to supporting regional countries' goal of flexible non-alignment.

Yet threading the needle between a deeper alliance with the United States and closer strategic relations with South-East Asia is tricky, even for Wong, whose diplomacy with the region has been deft and vigorous. This challenge is typified by regional doubts about the AUKUS arrangement. The persistence of these concerns, more than two years after the September 2021 announcement, suggests a genuine disagreement between Australia and South-East Asia about how best to preserve regional security.

## The region's reactions to AUKUS

South-East Asia's diversity precludes a single "South-East Asian" perspective on an issue as divisive as AUKUS. The ten countries in the Association of Southeast Asian Nations (ASEAN) encompass huge contrasts in political systems (from boisterous democracies like the Philippines to autocracies such as Vietnam), levels of economic development (from wealthy Singapore to conflict-torn Myanmar) and geographic proximity to China (from confident, distant Indonesia to small, weak Laos). Within each country, too, there exists diverging strands of opinion, between publics and elites, and between foreign affairs and defence bureaucracies.

Despite this diversity, it's possible to sketch out a prevailing South-East Asian perspective on US–China competition, which explains the region's responses to AUKUS. While Canberra has seen Beijing's growing power and assertive behaviour as an urgent challenge, South-East Asian capitals are likewise anxious but do not necessarily consider China the primary cause for concern. Rather, they often see the United States and China as morally equivalent superpowers. In this worldview, the United States, as much as China, is perceived as instigating tensions or raising the risk of conflict. China is not necessarily liked – public opinion surveys bear this out – but it is seen as a fact of life to be accepted, rather than pushed back against or changed. As Singaporean prime minister Lee Hsien Loong put it memorably to Scott Morrison in 2021: "You need to work with [China]. It is going to be there, it is going to be a substantial presence." In economic terms, China is regarded as the most valuable external partner, increasingly in terms of investment as well as trade. By contrast, the United States under both the Trump and Biden administrations has retrenched from economic engagement with Asia, withdrawing from the Trans-Pacific Partnership Agreement and offering only the weak Indo-Pacific Economic Framework as compensation. The "ASEAN way" – consensus, non-interference and incremental

**Both South-East Asia and Australia worry that the post–Cold War order is being eroded**

multilateral cooperation – remains the sine qua non of regional diplomacy. Surprises and "minilateralism" – doing things in smaller groups of like-minded countries – are frowned on.

In different ways, both South-East Asia and Australia worry that the post–Cold War order that has served the region's growth and development so well is being eroded. Canberra would assess that the regional status quo has already changed for the worse, since at least 2012, as Beijing's behaviour has become more assertive and its military has rapidly modernised. In other words, balance has already been lost, and needs to be restored through investments such as AUKUS. By contrast, South-East Asian officials often present the regional status quo as favourable but facing growing headwinds from tensions between great powers. This disagreement – between those who seek to maintain the status quo and those who see it as in need of restoration – lies in the background of debates about AUKUS.

There are exceptions to this broad-brush picture. Vietnam and the Philippines, which face a direct threat from China in the South China Sea, accept the need for a US presence, possibly even an increased one, to maintain a military balance of power. In 2023, both took major steps to boost their relationships with the United States. Manila allowed Washington to access four new military sites in the country, and Hanoi upgraded its ties with Washington to a "Comprehensive Strategic Partnership". Singapore, too, has at times been more willing to overtly recognise the value of the US presence in the region. The perspectives of these countries are important, but they are in a minority within South-East Asia. Elsewhere, and above all in Indonesia – the region's largest and most important power – a more ambivalent attitude prevails.

Given South-East Asia's reluctance to overtly take sides in regional rivalries, negativity in the region about AUKUS was not surprising. At the most basic level, a splashy announcement that Australia would be supported by the United States and the United Kingdom to acquire – in the words of Vice Admiral Jonathan Mead, head of Australia's nuclear-submarine taskforce – "the most formidable defence capability one can procure" cut against the region's ingrained preferences for predictability, consultation and preservation of the status quo. That the three countries were all anglophone and members of the Five Eyes intelligence-sharing arrangement made it more concerning to the region than the Quad, which has evolved slowly and includes Japan and India, making it a more diverse group. Concerns about the possibility of a non-nuclear power acquiring nuclear technology for military use also played a role, although Wong's response to this was compelling: Australia has a good track record in this area and has committed to work with the International Atomic Energy Agency to ensure adherence to its non-proliferation commitments.

Indonesia's foreign ministry said it was "deeply concerned over the continuing arms race and power projection in the region" and called on Australia to "maintain its commitment towards regional peace, stability and security" – implying that AUKUS called this into question. According to the ABC, President Widodo "repeatedly and forcefully" objected to AUKUS during an ASEAN meeting in late 2021. Malaysia's prime minister and its foreign and defence ministers all voiced unease that AUKUS could precipitate a regional arms race and raise the risk of conflict. Indonesia's and Malaysia's foreign ministers even met and together expressed their concerns about arms-racing and power projection.

Prime Minister Lee Hsien Loong issued a statement noting that Singapore "hoped that AUKUS would contribute constructively to the peace and stability of the region". Many commentators have taken this as an endorsement, but a close reading of Lee's careful words suggests that while Singapore is not necessarily anxious about AUKUS, it is reserving judgement on whether the partnership will be a net benefit to the region. The Philippines was the only country to make a genuinely positive statement, although Vietnam is often assumed to be supportive given its interest in checking China's naval power in the South China Sea. No other country made a public statement, but countries in mainland South-East Asia – such as Thailand and Cambodia – would almost certainly share the concerns expressed by Indonesia and Malaysia. In short, despite some exceptions, AUKUS was largely met with wariness or opposition in South-East Asia.

## Reservations about AUKUS

Despite the relative clarity of this response, Australia's understanding of regional perspectives on AUKUS has often been muddled. The first common misunderstanding is that South-East Asian countries are mere mouthpieces for Beijing. Certainly, China has portrayed AUKUS as undermining nuclear non-proliferation standards, in what the US State Department has said amounts to a disinformation campaign. China has also played on regional concerns about minilateralism by conflating AUKUS with the Quad and decrying both as examples of "bloc politics" that heighten polarisation in the region. Confusingly, Malaysia's former defence minister declared his intention to travel to Beijing for consultations with China on the AUKUS arrangement. But to assume that PRC disinformation is the source of the region's concerns about AUKUS wishes away the genuinely different strategic outlook of South-East Asian countries that underpins their responses.

**Australia's overriding preoccupation with the threat posed by China has not been lost on Jakarta**

A second misconception dismisses the region's publicly stated concerns about AUKUS because privately expressed views, especially among defence officials and personnel, have been more positive. It's true that the United States remains the region's most important defence partner, as a source of both kit and expertise. South-East Asian defence officials are thus more favourably disposed to Washington than their foreign ministry counterparts, who tend to be more receptive to China's economic influence. As Indonesian analyst Evan Laksmana has noted, publicly expressed concerns could in fact be more truthful, given that defence officials might provide assurances behind closed doors of their support for US strategic goals, in the hope of obtaining military sales and expertise from Washington and its allies. Perhaps to this end, Indonesia's defence minister at the time of the AUKUS announcement, Prabowo Subianto, was much more positive about AUKUS than its foreign minister, Retno Marsudi. Prabowo noted in a public forum in 2021 that he understood and respected the intentions behind AUKUS. Likewise, in 2023 President Widodo said that the Quad and AUKUS should be seen as "partners, not competitors" – a comment cited by Albanese in his Shangri-La Dialogue address. However, while positive for Australia, Widodo's riffing to reporters should not be interpreted as authoritative declaratory policy; in 2018, in an equally polite and baffling moment, he told an Australian newspaper that he hoped Australia would join ASEAN, even though in reality Indonesia would never support this.

A third misconception is that South-East Asia objected to AUKUS merely because it was not consulted or forewarned of the announcement. Indonesia did feel particularly aggrieved by this as the regular "two plus two" meeting of its defence and foreign ministers with their Australian counterparts was held just the week beforehand. Australia kept quiet despite the 2006 Lombok Treaty, signed by the two countries with the explicit purpose of establishing deeper consultation on security issues. This secrecy also occurred despite efforts by both sides to establish a culture of consultation and overcome a challenging history of mistrust and suspicion, particularly following Australia's role in supporting independence for East Timor. Forewarning would have helped, but it is unlikely it would have prevented objections entirely.

It's important to note, though, that while Jakarta is wary that AUKUS (and other Australian policy decisions) makes it more likely that Indonesia will be physically and politically caught in the middle of a regional conflict, it mostly does not regard itself as a target of AUKUS. Paranoid thinking about Australian intentions in Papua still exists in some pockets and online. Yet Australia's overriding preoccupation with the threat posed by China has not been lost on Jakarta. The concern in Indonesia is not so much that nuclear-powered submarines would be used against it, but that it may be drawn into a conflict by virtue of its archipelagic geography – the hinge between the Indian and Pacific oceans and between Australia and the world.

Interpretations that downplay the extent of disagreement between Australia and South-East Asia about AUKUS have found fertile ground in Australia, because many of us would rather not accept the uncomfortable truth that we simply do not see the world the same way as our neighbours.

## Australia's AUKUS diplomacy

South-East Asian views – no matter how deeply held – will not deter Canberra from pursuing AUKUS. For many defence officials and analysts, Indonesia's approval would be nice to have, but Canberra should not be prevented from doing what it must to safeguard the country's security. Why, they ask, should squeamish South-East Asian countries have a veto on the actions of those, like Australia, who are prepared to invest in maintaining a regional balance of power?

Even so, the Albanese government clearly still cares about how South-East Asia sees Australian strategic policy, including AUKUS. (The extent to which the Morrison government, which was more exclusively preoccupied with the Pacific, cared is less clear.) Led by Wong, Australia has ramped up a determined campaign of regional reassurance. In the wake of AUKUS, the Department of Foreign Affairs and Trade established new diplomatic positions overseas in important missions, such as those in Jakarta and Kuala Lumpur, to represent Australian strategic policy and report reactions, a costly exercise. The department's AUKUS arm is now called the AUKUS Defence Capability and Regional Engagement Branch, signalling this desire to engage with Australia's neighbours as part of its AUKUS diplomacy.

The government has increased its "pre-briefing" of South-East Asian countries ahead of defence announcements – so much so that regional officials are occasionally complaining that the briefings are excessive and becoming a nuisance. Ahead of the March 2023 announcement about the agreed "optimal pathway" for AUKUS, which included the decision to host a rotational presence of UK and US nuclear-powered submarines, the Albanese government said it made more than sixty phone calls to leaders, defence ministers and foreign ministers, in addition to a visit by Chief of the Defence Force Angus Campbell to key regional countries.

Officials are not unduly optimistic about the outcome of this diplomacy: they do not expect to convert Indonesia or Malaysia into a pro-AUKUS camp. Yet they hope that by communicating clearly and consistently, they may at least mitigate some of the region's sharpest concerns. Measured against these modest goals, Australian diplomacy post-AUKUS has been highly effective. Regional expressions of concern about AUKUS have not escalated, and AUKUS has not been criticised by ASEAN as a group: a statement issued by Brunei following an ASEAN meeting with Australia in October 2021 noted dully that during the meeting "views were expressed" about the implications of AUKUS for the region.

At the same time, the Albanese government has continued the efforts of previous Australian governments to establish deeper and more ongoing dialogue with regional countries; for example, pursuing a new agreement on defence cooperation and additional dialogues with defence and foreign ministry officials. Albanese was upbeat about this work in his 2023 Lowy Lecture, spruiking progress on a new defence cooperation agreement with Indonesia as "remarkable". These forums, although not explicitly about AUKUS, could enable a more mature conversation with the region that goes beyond a battery of pre-briefings. Though regional officials presumably prefer consultation to surprises, ad hoc pre-briefings by diplomats who are not subject-matter experts on defence policy risk delivering talking points that are repetitive, formulaic and poorly targeted.

What has been missing is a clear explanation from the Albanese government of why it seeks to acquire nuclear-powered submarines. Just as it has declined to elaborate on the practical purpose of AUKUS to its domestic audience, the government has also been circumspect to the region. In his Shangri-La Dialogue address – a major opportunity to set out Australian strategic policy – Albanese described nuclear-powered submarines as reflecting Australia's determination to "be a stronger partner and a more effective contributor to stability in our region". While there are legitimate reasons for circumspection, this kind of banal non-statement reassures no one.

Instead of seeking to reassure the region about the purpose of the nuclear-powered submarines, Australia has tended to focus more on the model way it is pursuing this technology. One word has resurfaced time and time again in this narrative: transparency. The March 2023 "optimal pathway" announcement noted the AUKUS countries were committed to "open and transparent engagement with partners within and beyond the region". Australian officials frequently highlight the contrast between AUKUS and China's military modernisation, which lacks transparency. Yet it's unclear if transparency alone is a winning message in South-East Asia.

A second plank of Australian defence officials' narrative is that AUKUS is not a "normative" arrangement which seeks to shape the region, but a simple technology-sharing partnership and a natural extension of the close relationships that have long existed between the three member countries. This is in contrast, for example, to the Quad, whose members have explicitly said they are setting out a vision for the Indo-Pacific region. While the Quad puts out statements on preferred approaches to issues such as technology governance, AUKUS does not. As a result, the reasoning goes, South-East Asian countries have no need to fear that AUKUS is eroding the central position of ASEAN in the region's multilateral architecture. Although this is true, all three AUKUS partners have at times undermined this claim with ambitious references to shared values and maintaining a free and open Indo-Pacific. If AUKUS has such lofty aims, then the region is less likely to see it as a simple technology-sharing agreement.

A third plank in Australia's defence of AUKUS relates to the unique advantages of nuclear-powered submarines in protecting Australia's vast coastline. Yet Australia has also given mixed signals about the purpose of the submarines, with some officials and analysts referring to the need for Australia to project power further north. Other defence officials have argued that changes in military technology mean that a hard distinction between defending Australia and projecting power further afield is no longer valid – nuclear-powered submarines can be deployed to advantage in both theatres. Official Australian defence planning documents argue that Australia's security and that of our region are inextricably linked – in other words, Australia's focus is not solely on defending its own territory, but on playing a more ambitious role in the region. Neither the Morrison nor Albanese governments have been willing to elaborate on the purpose to which nuclear-powered

**What has been missing is a clear explanation from the Albanese government of why it seeks to acquire nuclear-powered submarines**

submarines will be put. This is a challenge for Australia's narrative in the region as much as it is domestically.

While Australian diplomacy has been vigorous in private, Foreign Minister Wong has said little publicly about AUKUS during her extensive travel in the region. When she has spoken, Wong has tended to downplay the significance of AUKUS; for example, describing nuclear-powered submarines as "not a new capability for the region", and the arrangement as "an evolution of our relationships with the US and the UK". The lack of elaboration is deliberate, based on the calculation that public advocacy could precipitate further negative commentary from regional governments. This is a valid concern: when Wong made her first official visit to Malaysia, the then Malaysian foreign minister did not raise AUKUS but was effectively forced to restate Malaysia's position when prompted by a question from a reporter.

Opting for quiet, behind-the-scenes diplomacy is also logical given that AUKUS is largely an elite preoccupation. Opinion polling in the region suggests that few people are aware of AUKUS: a survey conducted by the Lowy Institute in Indonesia in 2021 found that just 11 per cent of Indonesians had heard of AUKUS.

That AUKUS has little public resonance in South-East Asia has helped to insulate Australia's bilateral relationships from any adverse impact. Wong's diplomacy has changed the tone of Australia's engagement, focusing on support for the region's priorities, especially in terms of economics, rather than counterproductive messaging on the threat posed by China. The Albanese government's South-East Asia economic strategy, launched in September 2023, is well targeted, if lacking in concrete action. With the exception of conflict-torn Myanmar, Australia has no disputes of note with the region and is at the forefront of the current frenzy to rebadge and upgrade relationships as "comprehensive", "strategic" or "comprehensive strategic". In fact, Australia's relationships with ASEAN and its members are arguably better than they've ever been.

## The widening gap between Australia and the region

Australia, then, should take South-East Asian perspectives on AUKUS not as a hot button issue to be managed or minimised, but as a signal of genuine disagreement about the right way to mitigate the risk of conflict between the United States and China in the decades ahead. In the Pacific, while views of AUKUS are similarly ambivalent, Australia's direct influence and role as the region's most important partner mean that attitudes to Australia are shaped by more diffuse factors, especially positions and action on climate change. But in South-East Asia, where we are just one of many external partners, our approach to regional security issues such as AUKUS forms an important part of how we are seen.

Viewed in this context, the responses to AUKUS imply that genuine strategic alignment with most of the region is becoming more difficult for Australia and the United States. The majority of South-East Asia remains wary about policies that seek to constrain China or reassert US influence in the region. In many ways, this makes the concept of "security in Asia" a dead letter. Anyone who hopes that Jakarta's regional vision will align with Canberra's on anything more than the lowest common denominator – a peaceful and prosperous region governed by rules – will be waiting for a long time. South-East Asia – apart from the Philippines – will largely hold back from joining the rapidly growing web of security cooperation among the United States and its allies, especially Australia and Japan.

The consequences for Australia's foreign and strategic policy are far-reaching. In the event of a conflict over Taiwan – the region's most dangerous flashpoint – the best that Australia could hope for would be South-East Asia remaining neutral. AUKUS has revived a longstanding debate in Indonesia about the use of its archipelagic sea lanes in a time of war, with some voices calling for Jakarta to refuse transit to Australian nuclear-powered submarines. This would be deeply concerning to Australia, given its enduring interest in freedom of movement for both military and commercial vessels through the archipelago. International lawyers argue such a move would not be valid under the UN Convention of the Law of the Sea, and experts doubt that the Indonesian navy has the practical capacity to enforce this. But it is telling that this idea appeals to those in Indonesia who worry about being drawn into a conflict among major powers.

In less drastic scenarios too, Canberra needs to be wary about the consequences of a South-East Asia that is essentially unsympathetic to its strategic worldview. Together with the islands of Melanesia, maritime South-East Asia encompasses our northern approaches, leading to the often-recited cliché that security threats to Australia, whether traditional or non-traditional, pass through South-East Asia. We cannot predict with confidence what will transpire in our region in the coming decades. Yet in any plausible scenario that we might imagine, Australia would be better informed and with greater scope for influence and action in pursuit of its own interests if it enjoyed mutual trust and close strategic relations with South-East Asia, especially Indonesia.

## Living with divergence

In managing this emerging difference in outlook with South-East Asia, Australia will be relatively alone among the AUKUS partners. For the United Kingdom and the United States, South-East Asia is just one of many regions they must prioritise. The Biden administration has accorded a high priority to its traditional alliance relationships in the Indo-Pacific, especially with the Philippines, but has given less attention to the rest of South-East Asia, especially Indonesia. Biden did not attend the 2023 ASEAN Summit hosted by Indonesian president Widodo. Unlike other recent US non-attendance at such summits, his absence was not explained by a crisis at home; this time, Indonesia and ASEAN were simply not sufficiently compelling to warrant presidential travel.

Australia, by virtue of its geography, has a long-term challenge: to reconcile a China-focused strategic policy of greater enmeshment with the United States with a desire for closer relations with its South-East Asian neighbours, following the Keating-era vision of "security in Asia". AUKUS makes this vision more difficult to achieve, because it increases the risk of a worst-case scenario in which Australia is seen as an anglophone outlier, playing an outsized role in defence and security issues while bringing little to the table in terms of economic cooperation. Defeating this perception is possible, but it would require broader investment in the non-defence aspects of Australia's relations with South-East Asia – for example, business and education links, as well as development assistance.

What Evan Laksmana has described as a growing "strategic divergence" between Australia and South-East Asia has largely been caused by rapid shifts in Australian policy over the past decade. Since 2011, Australian policy (like that of other US allies in the region, such as Japan) has changed radically – embracing an increased US presence in Australia, moving clearly to identify China as a threat, and seeking to project force at greater distance, including through AUKUS. Over the same period, the strategic policies of most South-East Asian countries have been largely static.

This divergence puts the onus on Australia to initiate and lead a much deeper dialogue with South-East Asian countries about the security choices it is making, and why. Unfortunately, this kind of conversation with our neighbours will only be possible once we've started to have it at home. ■

# PIT STOP POWER

## How to use our geography

Elizabeth Buchanan

AUKUS offers a once-in-a-generation defence capability of immense promise – a conventionally armed, nuclear-powered submarine (known as an SSN, "SS" for submarine and "N" for nuclear-powered). But, as it stands, the AUKUS pathway is unnecessarily complicated and is unlikely to deliver its main prize. It also misses an opportunity to exploit our strategic edge – our "pit stop power".

Australia embodies what Robert D. Kaplan dubs the "revenge of geography". Our island continent – rich in natural resources, with arable land and vast spaces – is an enviable piece of real estate. We should be framing our strategic value to our AUKUS partners in these geographical terms, thereby weaponising our latent pit stop power to our advantage.

This pit stop concept is based on an important – but sometimes overlooked – feature of car racing, defined by the *Collins Dictionary* as "a stop in the pits during a race, in which a competing car receives gasoline, a change of tires, or other servicing or repair". Or more generally (and informally) as "any brief stop during a trip so that one may get refreshments or use a restroom". Both definitions capture the broad requirements of any foreign vessel utilising Australian ports. For any state, it is essential to sustain operational needs while deploying force far from shore. From food, water and fuel to medical, maintenance and sewage, and everything in between, a pit stop is required.

Australia is a natural pit stop – well versed in sustaining and supporting allies and partners in our ports and airfields. Indeed, not just like-minded states: China and Russia have both used Hobart as a pit stop to Antarctica. The 2014 memorandum of understanding between China and Australia, Cooperation in the Field of Antarctic and Southern Ocean Affairs, signed by then prime minister Tony Abbott and President Xi Jinping, formalised arrangements between the two nations across enhanced logistics support and Tasmanian port access. In 2023, icebreakers from Italy and Germany made their first visits to Australia for their Antarctic programs. France and China also made pit stops in Hobart for 2023–24 Antarctic activities.

The rotation of allies, partners and like-minded states in and out of Australian ports provides a continued presence of capabilities in the Indo-Pacific to assist in shaping the region and maintaining the rules-based order that Australia values. A coherent strategy could lead to a pool of partners ready to sub in and out of our bases and ports to build a network which maintains stability in times of peace and helps project power in times of war. Looking beyond the current era in which the United States acts as the guarantor of stability and prosperity in the Indo-Pacific, supporting all advocates of the rules-based order bolsters Australian security options should Washington prove unreliable in the future.

## Australia: Hostess with the (SNN) mostest

Australia's pit stop power is already evident in the long record of partner SSN visits to our ports. Not just by the United States and the United Kingdom, but by France too. The first US SSN came in 1960 – the USS *Halibut*, which, en route to Australia, became the first SSN to successfully launch (somewhere in the Pacific) a guided missile.

Foreign SSN visits have ebbed and flowed with strategic competition. While US SSNs have consistently docked in Australia since the 1960s, the UK's first SSN visit was not until 1993. Aside from hosting foreign SSNs for decades, Australia has a track record of safely dealing with nuclear assets. Take, for example, the past sixty-five years (and counting) of our safely operating and maintaining a nuclear reactor at Lucas Heights, in New South Wales. Operational since 1958, this nuclear reactor is about 38 kilometres from the steps of the Sydney Opera House.

To capitalise on our pit stop power, we need to grow it. Our allies and partners have vital strategic interests in the Indo-Pacific maritime theatre. Global economic security is tied to trade with and through the Indo-Pacific region, home to 60 per cent of the world's population and set to be the heart of global growth for the coming century. This necessitates a consistent presence and credible power. Navy bases on the east and west coasts of Australia allow like-minded partners to deliver on our mutual interests in maintaining the liberal rules-based order at sea. Here, the AUKUS plan to stand up a Submarine Rotational Force-West (SRF-W) is a good start. SRF-W will be based at HMAS Stirling, in Western Australia. Royal Australian Navy personnel will deploy on the US and UK boats which rotate through the program, and maintenance personnel will start to support these boats while in port. Australians are smart and technologically capable – SRF-W is the first step to grow the workforce to sustain, maintain and operate SSNs out of our pit stop.

Not everyone grasps our pit stop power. Arguments that we are sacrificing our sovereignty by allowing US and other naval visits reveal a misunderstanding of the building blocks of Australia's defence capability: it is already mostly made in the United States. The existing intricate web of defence ties means that Australia requires a degree of coalition support to mount a combat division. In some ways this is the cost of Australian security interests, offset against a (comparatively) small population, with a finite budget, expected to patrol and secure an enormous swathe of ocean – the third-largest marine jurisdiction in the world.

Pillar One of AUKUS – aka the trilateral effort to support Australia to acquire conventionally armed SSNs – does not set out to cede Australian sovereignty. Canberra exercises plenty of strategic choice in its relationship with Washington, despite claims to the contrary.

Not all US requests for defence support are actioned by Australia, and the reality is that Washington values Canberra's voice (and agency) in international affairs. Without Australia, the US would have limited ability to shape and engage with Asia. Washington often works *through* Canberra.

SRF-W and any associated initiatives would remain under Australian control, consistent with bipartisan policy on foreign bases. Even the much-lauded US Pine Gap installation operates on the proviso that the Australian government is well within its rights to evict Uncle Sam – with twelve months' notice. Australia receives plenty of critical intelligence from the various US installations. We also gain from the operations enabled by US forces throughout the Indian and Pacific oceans based on activities undertaken on our shores. These benefits include the early warning of hostile intent, weather activity and military modernisation activities in our region, as well as efforts that support mutual values like the promotion and protection of international law and the rules-based liberal order.

**The range of activities which a pit stop enables is vast**

Some believe we are bound to a future of US domination if we go further down the AUKUS path. There are concerns that the US might leave us high and dry one day. But this is the situation already and has been since we inked the ANZUS Treaty in 1951. Australia is not afforded any protection by Washington; the treaty merely commits to a consultation. For the past seventy-plus years, we've operated alongside the US knowing full well it is not formally obliged to defend or assist Australia in times of need, nor has it promised that any response will have a military dimension. We've existed quite comfortably in a transactional relationship with Washington because we have a mutual interest in the defence of regional stability and unimpeded maritime flows.

Likewise, concerns that fashioning ourselves as a pit stop power for our allies would somehow place a target on Canberra's back overlooks the vast amount of real estate already occupied by Washington, from Darwin to Pine Gap to the North West Cape. It also betrays an undervaluing of the deterrent value embodied by hosting and supporting US military might. Besides, Australia must give a little to continue to live in the prosperous manner we have largely enjoyed, perhaps even taken for granted, in the post–World War II era. Opening our ports and expanding our hosting duties to partners beyond the AUKUS paradigm – such as France, Japan and India – is also worthy of consideration. As Lord Casey once quipped, "Every country's foreign policy is a compromise with that of its friends, and especially its strong friends." Indeed, only friendless states are *independent*.

## Where to sink our money

An enhanced pit stop approach requires plenty of infrastructure and facilities. Our ports (both current and proposed) would need sufficient wharfs, secure and ample storage, perhaps helicopter pads or airstrips, accommodation quarters, medical precincts and even respite facilities such as pools. Supplies of fuel, food and water are also critical for any pit stop, as is the disposal of waste such as sewage.

A pit stop port would support advanced maintenance and training capabilities for Australian trades, and facilitate interoperable servicing for boats – upskilling, raising and sustaining an entire domestic industry. From parts to tools and best-practice repairs, Australia's technologically savvy industrial workforce would have an excellent future. A pit stop would also need to provide surveillance of maritime approaches into port and port area security, as well as reliable communications and intelligence offerings.

The range of activities which a pit stop enables is vast. There is a clear diplomatic boost by making more boats available to undertake humanitarian and disaster relief missions in the region, to transport goods and personnel to disaster zones, to deliver medical services to remote islands, to support search-and-rescue operations and to provide enhanced port visits (naval diplomacy). Policing activities are also facilitated, including countering economic coercion and responding to maritime border challenges.

Often we consider the limitations of being a middle power only in relation to the toolkit, overlooking our lack of people – a vital element to operating and utilising the toolkit. It is no secret that recruitment and retention in our defence sector is dismal. So, we need to think differently. Already, vast training programs in Australia are being funded – we just need young Australians to gain interest.

Highly skilled engineers, project managers, technicians, construction workers and electricians are going to be needed to support SSN visits and plans for enhanced interoperation maintenance programs. Submariners will still be needed, as will shore-based support and logistics personnel.

The risk associated with hosting nuclear-powered submarines (SSNs) in our ports has been misunderstood. First, safety. The technology and design of the reactor in a nuclear-powered submarine (at least in the US variant, which Australia plans to host and then one day use) is such that it is physically impossible for the reactor to explode like a bomb. The highest probability of an incident involving the reactor would occur when the unit is on full operation – at a range deeply submerged and far from coasts. Or, as a study commissioned by the Canadian parliament found, "the corollary is that the likelihood of a reactor accident is lowest when the consequence of that accident would be most serious".

What about waste? One advantage of nuclear-powered submarines is they do not require refuelling, so the idea that Australian ports would be handling nuclear waste is irrational. And no, the fuel can't be nicked and used for nuclear weapons either. You'd need to be enriching uranium to around 90 per cent, and the uranium in said reactors is closer to 50 per cent enriched.

Hosting more SSNs in Australian ports delivers a net gain for Canberra. We have the real estate our allies and partners need to deliver on our mutual, enduring interest in maintaining the free flow of maritime trade in the Indo-Pacific. AUKUS also offers an opportunity for Australia to bolster its own capability through acquiring nuclear-powered submarines. But this still doesn't mean the answer is SSN-AUKUS.

## Right capability

According to the International Institute for Strategic Studies, six states possess an SSN capability. The US has sixty-seven, Russia has thirty-one, China has twelve, the UK has ten, France has nine, and India has one. Critically, all these states are stakeholders in the Indo-Pacific theatre. For example, the UK's economic security relies upon sea lines of communication in South-East Asia, France has overseas territories in the south-west Pacific, and Russia has its Pacific Fleet in the Russian Far East.

The 2020 Defence Strategic Update unveiled a trinity of challenges in Australia's strategic environment: major power competition, unrelenting coercion and sweeping military modernisation efforts underway in the region. All three necessitate strong maritime capabilities.

And this is where the SSN shines – primarily through its operational agility. The SSN's "stealth" makes it more versatile compared to its diesel-electric cousin – from missions spanning intelligence gathering, reconnaissance and strategic deterrence to combat in wartime. The SSN also gets top scores for its virtually unlimited range when compared to a conventional diesel-electric submarine. It can operate for extended periods without the need to surface, which reduces the risk of detection. Quite useful for an isolated sea-bound nation like Australia.

The case for acquiring SSNs is bolstered by the reality that conventional (diesel-electric) submarines require a steady fuel supply. For Australia, our sea lanes – the arteries which connect us to the world (and the world to us) – are vital security interests to defend in the face of both war and peace. Yet our maritime capabilities tasked with defending these interests are reliant on fuel – fuel which relies on these functional arteries to arrive at our shores. Australia imports over 90 per cent of its diesel via these sea lanes. Possessing a vital capability in our defence toolbox that relies on insecure supply chains to even operate is nonsensical.

## Wrong pathway

The SSN is the right capability for a geographically isolated nation like Australia, but the current pathway to achieve it is problematic. Of course, future submarine planning is a popular pastime for Canberra. The process is as Australian as John Farnham. And, like Farnham, Australia's future submarine planning process returns to the stage every decade or two.

The 2009 Defence White Paper (DWP) articulated the strategic basis for a new submarine project. It shared the result of an internal review that found the Australian Defence Force needed to go from six to twelve submarines. The 2009 DWP also noted the future submarines needed greater range and endurance than the Collins class to be viable for the strategic environment expected by 2030.

In a random, disjointed line in the White Paper, nuclear-power propulsion was nixed as a possibility, which raises suspicion that there were indeed pointed deliberations over the utility of an SSN capability.

In the wake of the 2009 DWP, Canberra flirted with the Japanese on the future submarine project but, in the end, committed to the French. Given that one in three marriages end in divorce in our country, it should really come as little surprise that Canberra's union with Paris on the submarine project eventually ended. But France remains inextricably linked to Australia's security environment due to its territories throughout the Indo-Pacific. Perhaps this saga will be a masterclass in "conscious uncoupling", as the heat from Canberra's decision appears to have largely dissipated in Paris.

Australia walked away from the French and announced its new partnership – AUKUS – through which the next chapter of our submarine planning history is set to be written. So far, the pathway selected endeavours to deliver the ballyhooed SSN-AUKUS. The SSN-AUKUS will follow a UK design and feature US technology (comparable to the Virginia-class SSN) from weapons systems to navigation systems and, of course, nuclear propulsion. The boat is to be assembled and/or built in both the UK and Australia. The UK seeks to deliver its first domestically built SSN-AUKUS in the 2030s to the Royal Navy, with Australia looking to deliver its own domestically built SSN-AUKUS in the 2040s.

The SSN-AUKUS will be operated by the UK and Australia, with the US opting to maintain a unilateral approach via its own future submarine – the SSN-X. All three states plan to deliver a joint combat system specifically for the SSN-AUKUS. It is likely this system would feature in the SSN-X as well.

Washington will sell us three (or up to five) Virginia-class SSNs as a stop-gap solution while we wait for the arcane SSN-AUKUS. Potentially we will still be operating the conventional Collins-class at the same time, if the first Virginia-class boat arrives in the 2030s. The third key component of the agreed pathway is enhanced port visits to be facilitated by SRF-W. While US and UK SSNs won't be permanently based at SRF-W, it is likely they will remain at times for up to three months to undertake maintenance. We should expect only one UK SSN (Astute-class) to visit SRF-W, while up to four US SSNs (Virginia-class) will be hosted.

Legislative hurdles are already being overcome, clearing the way for the future SSN-AUKUS. The US has agreed to share elements of its "crown jewels" related to nuclear propulsion with Canberra – only ever shared once before, with London. This is no small feat. Agreements on naval personnel, nuclear-reactor safety and servicing as well as SSN maintenance training packages have been inked between the partners. And Australian sailors are embedded already in US and UK SSN operations.

Immense industrial base investments are also occurring, with the UK injecting £4 billion into three domestic firms to design the SSN-AUKUS. Closer to home, the Department of Defence has earmarked prime industrial real estate in South Australia for expanded shipbuilding (and/or assembly) enterprises. Canberra has also promised

$3 billion over the next five years to enhance US shipyard capacity. Further, dates have been established for SRF-W to come online, with UK and US SSNs to begin arriving under its auspices from 2027 and 2029, respectively.

The current plan does enhance (at least in words) avenues for interoperability with the UK and US. Indeed, more (friendly) SSNs in the Indo-Pacific could share the burden associated with the maintenance of our rules-based order. Their presence would ensure the free flow of the sea lanes which promote stability in the region, and help to keep adversaries far from our shores.

**The SSN-AUKUS probably won't materialise**

Further, this pathway also promises to turbocharge Defence capability and enhance the respective industrial sectors of the three AUKUS members. Some gain more than others, but surely we aren't naive enough to believe all partners are equal. Washington gains more boats on station in the region and ports that are beyond Beijing's (current) strike ability as well as investment in its shipyards. The UK will also gain economically with injections into its shipbuilding sector, as will British defence firms that sign contracts to build or assemble boats in South Australia.

Of course, very little of this is news. The US is an old hand at using Australia for military operations – just look to World War II, in which Australia provided a valuable position to launch from, notably

Washington's missions to New Guinea and the Philippines. Further, Fremantle was the second-largest Allied submarine port in the Pacific theatre during World War II, just behind Pearl Harbor.

Port calls have long been a facet of normal naval operations for Washington in the region, with the US Seventh Fleet making 102 port visits to Australia in 1997 alone. Indeed, the bilateral relationship has long been anchored by military training and exercise schedules, clearly moving towards interoperability.

It would seem that chasing a fully sovereign defence capability is imprudent. Australia has never really been self-reliant, but nor has it been disadvantaged by this. Self-reliance in Australian defence terms will happen, to borrow the words of Julia Gillard, "not now, not ever". Point is, it is not necessarily a bad thing for Australian security.

Leaning into our pit stop power will ensure Australia remains a relevant, valued facilitator of US regional power for the foreseeable future. The increased presence in the Indo-Pacific of allied and partner SSNs, continually utilising our ports, injects a semblance of stability into an otherwise uncertain and ever-changing strategic environment.

## The SSN-AUKUS fallacy

But there is an elephant in the room, even though it is not a concern for current AUKUS leaders and key backers because it won't need attention for a decade or so. Nonetheless, the quandary exists, and we should acknowledge it: the SSN-AUKUS probably won't materialise.

Domestic tensions in both the US and UK are simmering away, with Washington already stating it has no plans to ever operate the boat.

Domestic politics is a constant "known unknown" for any defence acquisition or foreign policy plan. But the political will in Washington is not behind the SSN-AUKUS; it is not the future boat of the US Navy. There are further concerns about the US domestic capacity to deliver the Virginia-class SSNs to Australia. Could the partners find a way to deliver on Pillar One intent without pursuing the SSN-AUKUS? Here, the US's SSN-X is worth further probing.

Pillar One does have elements worth salvaging. The sale by Washington to Canberra of at least three Virginia-class SSNs from as soon as the early 2030s is reasonable. As is the exchange of expertise through the embedding of personnel and injection of capital into shipyard infrastructure. Increasing SSN visits to Australian ports by our UK and US partners via the SRF-W is also sensible. Indeed, the SRF-W should be put on steroids.

But the design and attempted construction of a future submarine – the SSN-AUKUS – should be scrapped. This would save us time and money, given the high likelihood that the SSN-AUKUS won't eventuate. With the US not intending to operate the SSN-AUKUS and committing to the SSN-X instead, Canberra is left to rely on London. This is precarious to say the least.

Since Federation, Australia has marched to the drumbeat of the Western maritime power of the day – once the UK and now, since World War II, it is US power that matters, particularly as strategic competition increases in the Indo-Pacific. Of course, competition in our neck of the woods is overwhelmingly maritime in nature.

It follows that Canberra should focus its efforts on interoperability with the US in our maritime backyard. After all, Washington is geographically wedded to the same Pacific arena. It is clear our long-term regional maritime interests align more with Washington than with London. And from a cursory look at the UK maritime toolbox, this is perhaps smart policy too.

## Charting the right course to the SSN

A viable approach to correcting our current SSN pathway begins with recognising our pit stop power. We should acquire as intended the three Virginia-class subs and get behind the US's SSN-X. If the UK fulfils the ambitious SSN-AUKUS project, it will likely share similar elements to the SSN-X in any case – not least the weapons and propulsion systems. Theoretically, Australia would provide maintenance and support for the UK's SSN-AUKUS via SRF-West, as we will for the Virginia-class subs and probably for the SSN-X too.

This more sensible AUKUS pathway takes advantage of Australia's pit stop power. Our value proposition to partners is our enhanced ability to maintain and host their SSN capabilities, while also bringing our own capabilities to the table – our highly skilled workforce and innovative defence industry. Come 2030 and through to the 2040s, Australia's SRF-W is likely to contain no less than five different submarine classes. We could see our trusty but aged Collins-class aside a single visiting

British Astute, up to nine Virginias (if Australia receives all five and up to four US boats visit), as well as the SSN-X and, of course, the mystical SSN-AUKUS.

This is surely more submarine capability housed in the Indo-Pacific than the AUKUS partners could poke a stick at, which is good news for Canberra. Keeping the waters of the Indo-Pacific free from coercion, disruption and potentially armed conflict is a binding mutual interest for Australia, the US and the UK. This is also true for Australia's global partners and allies, as maritime security challenges originating in the Indo-Pacific ripple to all ends of the Earth.

Of course, our competitors – and states we don't see eye to eye with – also want the continued facilitation of maritime trade throughout the world. But the capabilities to marshal and control the world's seas are strengthening and not necessarily in our favour, with vast military modernisation processes underway in our neighbourhood, from China to India.

## One ping only, please

In the wise words of Sean Connery's naval captain in *The Hunt for Red October*, "one ping" tells us only part of the picture. The optimal pathway tabled by AUKUS leaders is merely *one* approach to SSN capability for Australia. There are many options for achieving the right capability. We've committed to a pathway that has welcomed extremely limited consultation or public debate. One ping, one approach, tells only part of the picture.

Defence acquisition is an enduring process, involving constant review and revision. But even a capability novice must accept that pursuing a "Frankenstein" approach to delivering an SSN is beyond the pale in terms of risk.

This is not a call to walk back on the plan to acquire nuclear-powered submarines. Indeed, we should crack on with buying three (or five) Virginia SSNs and perhaps commit to the SSN-X once the cost is more sensible for Canberra. For now, we are on the wrong pathway to the right capability.

As the island continent smack bang in the middle of the Indian and Pacific ocean theatres, Australia cannot bunker down and avoid the fallout of sharpening competition on its doorstep. But nor should Canberra *expect* to sidestep said competition. As a net beneficiary of the extant rules-based order, secured and administered primarily by our partners (read: Washington), Australia ought to be providing security too. Committing to host more SSNs in the Indo-Pacific frees up Washington's capacity to shape environments elsewhere, which is also often in our interest.

Our pit stop power is a potential solution to a glaring problem: the SSN-AUKUS might not ever eventuate. While this would not necessarily be detrimental to Australia, we nonetheless need an SSN capability. We can arrive at one by putting SRF-W at the centre of AUKUS, making the most of our pit stop power to support the enhanced operation of partner SSN presence in our backyard, while continuing efforts to acquire and operate our own SSN capability. Any optimal pathway surely needs to be sensible, too. ■

# SUNK COSTS

## Our high-stakes gamble on nuclear-powered submarines

Andrew Davies

The AUKUS agreement provides Australia with a pathway to a war-fighting capability that previously seemed out of reach: nuclear-powered submarines, which are a big step-up from the navy's current fleet of conventionally powered boats. But there are substantial – and perhaps under-appreciated – strategic, industrial and budgetary risks. And it will be very expensive, especially when opportunity costs to the broader economy are taken into account.

As junior partners on the submarine program, Australia will be reliant on the continued willingness of the United States and the United Kingdom – over many decades – to help us build, operate and sustain our new capability. The apparent determination to build submarines locally only increases the challenges. Domestic naval shipbuilding has a mixed history, with poor outcomes as frequent as good ones in the past forty years. Most programs have run late, over budget or both.

The best-case scenario is that we acquire a world-class submarine capability that provides us with hitherto unobtainable levels of independent deterrence, enhancing our ability to project power while building a robust new skill set in Australian industry in the process. The worst case is that we spend hundreds of billions of dollars, diverting scarce industrial assets from the productive part of the economy into an orphan sector, and end up with little extra military muscle. And, if we fail to achieve a sufficient level of sovereignty, we could effectively be locked into whatever strategy Washington chooses to pursue in the western Pacific – or indeed be stranded if US policy takes a turn away from active international involvement. It's a high-stakes gamble. So, are we likely to win?

## A new class of submarine

Moving to a fleet of nuclear-powered attack submarines (abbreviated "SSNs" in naval nomenclature) represents a significant policy shift for Australia. For decades, SSNs were in the too-hard basket, and those who suggested them were usually shot down quickly. The most frequent objections were that all the countries that fielded nuclear submarines also had a substantial nuclear power industry that provided the pool of skills and regulatory frameworks required to operate such complex machines, and that nuclear submarine technologies were such closely guarded secrets that not even our closest allies would share them with us.

Nonetheless, Australia has long wanted many of the operational characteristics of nuclear-powered submarines. If we were to focus only on defending Australian territory and our immediate approaches, submarines aren't the weapons of choice, with aircraft and missile systems being more cost-effective. But because submarines are much harder to detect than surface vessels or aircraft, they can operate in forward areas with less risk, so they are best suited for threatening an adversary's assets and collecting information far from our shores. Thus, during and since the Cold War, the Royal Australian Navy's Oberon-class and later Collins-class submarines ranged far and wide across the western Pacific. But the low speeds of diesel-electric submarines meant that many days were spent in long transits, so they could only maintain operational patrols for relatively short times. As well, conventional submarines tend to be smaller than their nuclear-powered cousins, so their payload of weapons and sensors was necessarily limited. With the much greater power density of nuclear fuel compared to diesel, SSNs can be larger – affording larger payloads – faster and with superior endurance. They are a good match for the nation's military requirements.

Having assumed that nuclear-powered submarines were denied to us, Australia worked hard – and expended a lot of money – to produce unique conventional submarines that could stay at sea longer, and travel further and a bit faster than anyone else's. The Collins class – which entered service in 1996 – was a step in that direction, and the contract with France to build the follow-on Attack class, now cancelled in favour of the AUKUS arrangement, was even more ambitious. Had the project delivered as agreed, the Attack class would have been easily the largest, most complex (and consequently the most expensive) conventional submarines in the world – and would still have offered a performance well below that of nuclear boats.

This explains the alacrity with which Australia took up the deal when access to nuclear-powered submarines was presented. By building upon decades of experience in American and British submarine programs, we avoid the fraught process of designing and building a conventionally powered replacement for the Collins class and get a better submarine in the process. But that greater capability is expensive. The costs are high even by the standard of large defence projects, and SSNs will cost multiples of the $50 billion price tag of the Attack class.

## It's all about China

The Australian people might reasonably ask why we need such expensive assets. What threat is dire enough to warrant the hundreds of billions of dollars that could otherwise be spent on education, health or welfare? No discussion of the proposed nuclear-powered submarines can ignore the strategic questions of how, where and against whom they might operate. Based on public statements by successive governments, most recently in the 2023 Defence Strategic Review, about a "deteriorating strategic environment", it's clear that the submarines are intended to hedge against the rising military power and ambitions of China. No other regional country has the naval and missile forces required to credibly threaten Australia or to disrupt the established order. Much has been written on the potential threat posed by China, and it's not hard to find views that challenge the strategy of trying to balance its hard power. But Australia has decided that it is possible – and important enough – to warrant large expenditures.

If balancing China is the objective, then the endeavour makes the most sense in an ANZUS alliance context. Only the United States has forces that could match China's. But that gets more difficult as Chinese power grows, so for the US, having allies with capabilities that augment its own is highly desirable. Australian submarines that have much in common with US boats (and the first three to five will actually be US Virginia-class boats) effectively add more alliance capacity in theatre. America doesn't have as many SSNs as it would like, so it would welcome a close ally footing the bill and adding extra submarines to the pool. But that would only work if Australia's submarines didn't come at the cost of slower deliveries to the US, so an expansion of submarine construction capacity is also required. The Australian plan to build submarines locally is consistent with that.

> **In the worst case, we might struggle to secure support for our submarines from a disengaged America**

Sovereignty is an important consideration here. If Australia becomes effectively tied to the US Pacific strategy through the submarines, then a couple of major risks arise. American adventurism or miscalculation could embroil us in a conflict not of our choosing. Alternatively, if the United States decides that military strategic competition in the western Pacific is no longer a priority, we could find ourselves with an expensive asset that no longer operates as part of a much larger fleet. In the worst case, we might struggle to secure support for our submarines from a disengaged America. Today a significant minority of the Republican Party seems to view alliances with deep suspicion rather than as assets. Given that, and the real prospect of another Trump presidency, relying on US policy remaining consistent and well considered over several decades seems imprudent. Of course, AUKUS also includes Britain, but the days when the Royal Navy had the wherewithal to deploy in force on this side of the world are far behind us.

So we need to think about the utility of Australian SSNs in a plausible future in which we can't rely on US support in meeting a military threat from China. Australia cannot raise forces that could defeat Chinese forces, but that isn't necessarily the aim. Deterrence essentially boils down to being able to credibly threaten an adversary with enough harm to outweigh any gains it might achieve. Whether a small number of SSNs can do this to offset the considerable cost of buying and sustaining them is difficult to judge, though they can put high-value targets such as aircraft carriers at risk.

Australia's current plan is to train crews on American and British submarines and then take delivery of three to five Virginia-class submarines from the US, starting in the early 2030s. Then construction of a new class of SSNs for Australia and the UK would begin in the late 2030s in the UK, and sometime after 2040 in South Australia. A rule of thumb is that three submarines are required for one to be operational at any given time, so with a final fleet size of eight by around 2050 we are realistically talking about at most two or three Australian submarines being active in theatre, and for most of the 2040s we would have even fewer. It's little wonder that analysts have raised the relative cost effectiveness of long-range aircraft and missile systems as alternatives.

## The cost

But Australia seems determined to press ahead. If we are to make the submarine project work, we need to deepen our own industrial capabilities. But that will add considerably to the cost – not just the direct costs of equipment, facilities and people, but also the indirect costs of diverting scarce national resources into an enterprise that will compete with more productive elements of the economy.

The best official figure we have for the project is "$268–368 billion" over the next thirty years (and more over the submarines' lifetime). That will make it by far our largest-ever defence project. (For comparison, the cost of buying our Joint Strike Fighters and operating them for twenty years will be around $30 billion.) Buying and running SSNs risks distorting the defence budget and requiring the ADF to make serious cuts elsewhere – thus losing flexibility in crises for which nuclear submarines are not helpful. A few years ago, analysis of the defence budget showed that the Attack-class price tag was already drastically reducing the funds available for other defence priorities, and the nuclear submarine project budget is more than five times larger. Without a dramatic increase in the defence budget, it's hard to see how it's going to fit.

And it's not clear that we can put much faith in even the fuzzy cost estimates we have. The US experience suggests caution – its navy has been struggling for years to fund the construction of America's own nuclear submarines, even with an annual budget of A$380 billion. One problem has been a bottleneck in production capacity in US shipyards, making it difficult to ramp up production even if funding is secured from Congress. It's challenging to grow a boutique industrial capability with no commercial equivalent, there being no export or civilian market for nuclear-powered submarines. A few years ago, the Pentagon thought a couple of billion would be enough to expand production, but that proved overly optimistic. Ultimately, the US would like to get three new Virginia-class SSNs out of its shipyards every year, but it has spent billions to reach two per year by 2028.

Australia is stumping up $4.7 billion to help the US boost production. That should help lock in access to the promised submarines, but if the US can't meet its own needs, its support for the AUKUS arrangement could still wane. In that case, keeping the Virginia-class boats earmarked for Australia might be preferable. Prime Minister Albanese's Washington trip in October 2023 saw AUKUS receive effusive support from the Biden administration, but support from

Republicans was more muted. While Congress voted in December to allow the export of Virginia submarines to Australia (passed 310–118 in the House), a future Congress might be receptive to an argument from the navy for reneging on, or at least delaying, aspects of the AUKUS arrangement, leaving us in a parlous position with few realistic options to bridge the gap.

## The industrial question

Supporting submarines is a highly specialised task, and the recent history of Australia's submarine fleet contains some salutary lessons. Our track record with conventional submarines – which require substantially fewer resources than nuclear ones – has been mixed at best.

We operated British-built Oberon submarines from 1969 to 2000 and the Collins class since. Local expertise was required to support – and later upgrade – the Oberons, and the supply of parts and services from the UK was sometimes problematic. The locally built Collins-class submarines were delivered without sufficient regard to their ongoing support, resulting in a poor fleet performance for a decade. The situation was remediated only after considerable effort and the infusion of more funds than initially allocated. In both cases we learnt the hard way that supporting these complex machines requires specialised expertise and substantial extra funding.

When we enter the SSN world, the challenges will increase. Nuclear attack submarines are among the most complicated machines in existence, requiring a substantial level of investment and expertise.

Not only are the boats larger and more complex than either predecessor class, but the nuclear-propulsion system brings its own technical and regulatory issues.

At one stage the US Navy was getting thirty-five operational days a year on average from each of its SSNs. And that is with decades of experience and the economies of scale possible from a much larger fleet than the eight we aspire to. American help will be critical, but we'll still have to pull our own weight. Getting the support arrangements right and appropriately resourced is not optional.

While we rely on US SSNs in the short term ("short" is a relative term here, being out to 2040), Australia might be able to get by without deep local industrial support. The US Navy routinely operates its own boats from Guam, performing only routine support tasks locally and returning them to the United States for deeper maintenance. We will do the same, avoiding the need for heavy investment in domestic support arrangements by piggybacking on services already in place for the US fleet, with the yards at Pearl Harbor maintaining our Virginia-class boats. The downside to that approach is the lack of sovereignty that comes with such an arrangement, and the possibility that, in a crisis or time of heightened tension, we could slide down the priority order for services at exactly the time we need them.

It's hard to see how a similar arrangement with the UK could function effectively. Because the Royal Navy, unlike the US Navy, has no Pacific base, the distances involved and the smaller size of the British submarine enterprise (the Royal Navy has ten submarines compared to the US's sixty-four) pretty much make that a non-starter. Eventually we'll need to be able to support submarines here. We can certainly do that if we're prepared to invest the necessary resources; we have world-class engineering skills in the resources sector, as well as the educational resources to train people for the work. Our AUKUS partners will allow Australians to work with them on their submarine programs, and naval personnel will serve on their submarines. Work is underway both inside and outside of the Department of Defence to develop a path towards a high level of self-sufficiency in submarine ownership.

So, we can support nuclear-powered submarines – but we shouldn't kid ourselves that this is going to be anything other than tremendously expensive. Big defence projects are often touted by politicians as an opportunity to boost the economy by providing jobs and bringing new skill sets into local industry. We can be sure that, as the biggest project of them all, it will be accompanied by many declarations of its value to the wider economy and of the number of jobs it will create.

However, it's hard to support that notion. The overlap between nuclear submarines and other economic activities in Australia is even less than for conventional submarines, so any gains will be marginal, despite the much higher costs. And in the absence of a nuclear power industry in Australia, there is no overlap at all between the management and regulation of nuclear technologies and other economic activity. The nuclear industries that the other operators of SSNs possess aren't necessary for maintaining the submarines, but they increase the number of positions and the depth of experience in the workforce.

As I showed in my previous AFA essay "Can Australia Fight Alone?", the defence industrial sector is a less efficient revenue producer than the rest of the Australian manufacturing sector, in which firms have identified a competitive niche. Diverting people into an expanded defence sector will tend to make the overall economy less efficient. And where there are overlaps in skilled trades, an increased demand for people will tend to drive wages up, thus reducing the efficiency of competing sectors. Building the industry to construct and adequately maintain nuclear-powered submarines might be worthwhile for strategic reasons, but it won't do much for the wider economy. No doubt the photo ops will be terrific, but the economic spin-offs are unlikely to be.

## And the clock is ticking ...

As noted earlier, it took over a decade to put adequate support arrangements in place for the Collins class after the delivery of the first boats from the Adelaide shipyards. And even after a substantial and costly remediation effort that saw availability levels finally reach international benchmarks, the nation's submarine capability still seems fragile. Breakdowns, flooding and fires have been reported in the past few years and some of the submarines have been in maintenance longer than planned.

Adequately crewing submarines has been a consistent problem for the navy. Any uptick in the resources sector typically spells trouble for navy retention rates, especially for critical trades like engineers. Considering that there are fifty-eight people in a Collins-class submarine and 135 in a Virginia class, a lot of effort will be needed to grow the workforce to crew even three Virginia-class boats in the 2030s. Even if the future UK/Australia submarines have smaller crews (current British boats have ninety-eight), crewing eights SSNs is going to be a real stretch for a navy still struggling to crew six Collins.

Meanwhile, the clock is ticking on the Collins class, despite a planned life-extension program to keep it competitive in the second half of the 2030s. By 2040 the youngest Collins submarine will be thirty-four years old. And many of the people best placed to manage the Collins are also needed to guide and plan the nuclear submarine project. And there won't be much wriggle room in the schedule – if the first SSNs aren't released by the US in time because of changed American priorities (or our perceived lack of readiness), or if the UK/Australian boats are delayed in construction, Australia might find itself in the "deteriorating strategic environment" that sparked all this with few or even no submarines in its deterrence posture.

**By 2040 the youngest Collins submarine will be thirty-four years old**

The level of commitment to AUKUS demonstrated by both major parties suggests that a significant change of direction is unlikely any time soon. The value of nuclear submarines comes down to being able to create a significant deterrent effect to Chinese adventurism by threatening important Chinese assets far from our shores, at a cost of hundreds of billions of dollars. That makes some sense if we're thinking only in terms of supporting a broader US-led effort, but it is much less clear when contemplated as an Australian stance. And the more we move away from a US-led strategy (or the US moves away from us), the more it will cost us to acquire all the elements required to operate independently, and the greater the opportunity costs will be to other approaches to managing Australia's future.

If we get this wrong – and that is a real possibility – we won't have time for a plan B. We've embarked on a high-stakes approach to strategic risk management, with little leeway for setbacks and little prospect of our spending on this enterprise paying us back in other ways. It is a real possibility that by the late 2030s we will be out of pocket to the tune of many billions of dollars and at greater strategic risk, with little tangible benefit. ■

# THE FIX *Solving Australia's foreign affairs challenges*

## Hervé Lemahieu on How Australia Can Unleash Its Own "Brussels Effect" in the Pacific Island Region

"There is much that Australia ... could learn from the political logic of early European integration for tackling the [Pacific] region's unique climate, economic and geopolitical challenges."

**THE PROBLEM:** Hardly a week goes by without a new initiative by Australia in the Pacific island region – involving more aid, more loans or more defence cooperation. Much of this effort is to beat China at its own game, responding to Beijing's "trade plus security" overtures with a blend of infrastructure, budget support and upgraded security arrangements. But increased aid and defence diplomacy can only go so far and will not change the fundamentals of a bidding war with China for the loyalty of Pacific island countries. Many continue to have every incentive to play the powers off against each other in a transactional manner.

Canberra policymakers often appear unable or unwilling to answer an essential question: what is the long-run strategy to break the wicked problem of playing "whack-a-mole" with China across the region?

The most compelling answer to encroaching Chinese influence is by changing the rules of engagement through an Australian policy that builds durable regional integration – one that would enmesh Pacific island countries, Australia and New Zealand into an EU-style project. That aspiration is not new and has led to false starts in the past.

But Australia has many cards left unplayed. It is formally a part of many Pacific regional processes and by far the largest member of the Pacific Islands Forum (PIF). Just as Germany has powered European integration while leading from behind on European diplomacy, so too could Australia for the Pacific island region.

European unity owes much to the strategic choices of France and Germany in the 1950s. They elected to remedy centuries of conflict on the European continent by radically technocratic means. The European project started with the creation of the European Coal and Steel Community in 1951, which pooled resources and infrastructure vital to industry and war. Integration in one sector then led to a "spillover" of technical cooperation in other policy areas. Another powerful catalyst of European integration was open borders, which allowed for the formation of something closer to a European identity among everyday citizens.

In the Pacific, too, necessity must be the mother of invention. Pacific island countries face a human-made calamity like no other in the form of climate change and rising sea levels, compounded by stagnant development, geographic fragmentation and the often corrosive influence of geopolitics on weak governance.

The region's collective ability to cope with this mix of circumstances is hampered by strict border policies restricting the movement of people and wealth, few economic complementarities among small island states, poor regulatory, financial and communications infrastructure, and inadequate and costly channels for overseas Pacific labourers sending money home – a critical source of Pacific household and national income.

There is much that Australia and New Zealand, the two most powerful PIF states, could learn from the political logic of early European integration for tackling the region's unique climate, economic and geopolitical challenges.

**THE PROPOSAL:** Australia has a unique ability to unleash its own "Brussels effect" in the Pacific, shaping the region through little more than its market size and regulatory standards.

This would require that it commit to – and progressively ease barriers on – the free movement of data, capital and people across the Blue Pacific Continent.

Australia should lead on two PIF–endorsed initiatives: the creation of a digital single market for the Pacific, and a phased expansion of the Trans-Tasman free travel area.

What coal and steel were to Europe in the 1950s, technology and telecommunications are to the Pacific today – at once a vector of geopolitical competition and a possible solution for it. Australia, New Zealand and their Pacific partners would have much to gain from pooling their telecommunication sectors to bridge the region's great digital divide.

A digital single market could help set supranational standards for secure and trustworthy digital infrastructure and services, and promote greater market access, competition and efficiencies through a common regulatory framework. But its ultimate aim would be to collapse geographic barriers by drastically lowering the costs of cross-border transfers of data and capital.

One way to do this is through a Pacific-wide framework for secure electronic identification (eID) and cashless payments. A Pacific eID system linked to a digital remittances app is needed to overhaul some of the world's highest transaction fees for sending remittances from Australia and New Zealand to Pacific island countries. This would be an investment in the financial infrastructure of the region and significantly boost national incomes. Initially targeted at Pacific labourers overseas and their families at home, the wider rollout of a common eID for all Pacific citizens would transform remote communities: from enabling online access to government services to participation in the formal and international banking sector.

An integrated digital market would also make it easier to end roaming charges for calls, text messages and accessing the internet for users from one PIF country travelling to or residing in another. This should begin by capping the wholesale rates that networks can charge each other to allow their subscribers access to their networks. Such an initiative would be a tangible demonstration of the benefits of belonging to one Pacific family, not least for the hundreds of thousands of tourists from Australia and New Zealand who visit Pacific island countries every year.

A shared digital ecosystem would pave the way for the most significant form of PIF integration possible: an EU-style common travel area for the Pacific. This may seem a distant reality, but a de facto one already exists in the form of the Trans-Tasman Travel Arrangement, which allows the nationals of a quarter of the PIF's member states – Australia, New Zealand, Cook Islands, Niue and Tokelau (a PIF associate member) – to live, work and study across each other's borders.

In the Pacific, the backbone of integration will be the movement of people rather than intra-regional trade.

Australia has shown new willingness to experiment on this front, including through a Pacific Engagement Visa and, far more significantly, by announcing a world-first climate mobility treaty with Tuvalu. The Falepili Union – allowing a small number of Tuvaluans, chosen by ballot, to be accepted as permanent residents in Australia per year – opens the doors for a more ambitious multilateral innovation.

Much as five European countries forged the Schengen Agreement of 1985, Australia and New Zealand – together with the three other PIF countries involved in the Trans-Tasman corridor – could merge several arrangements into one by establishing a treaty for the creation and expansion of a Pacific common travel area. Such an initiative would, like the Schengen Area, incentivise reforms in applicant states to allow for the lifting of restrictions on cross-border travel. Accession to the common travel area would be based on a set of criteria tailored to the region, including:

a) the integrity and security of an applicant state's border, immigration and citizenship controls; and

b) the compatibility of governance and economic standards in applicant states with those of existing members, particularly in terms of institutional stability, rule of law, and a requisite capacity to minimise brain drain.

Based on these conditions, the most developed economies in the Pacific, such as Fiji, would be first in the queue to join. However, full accession would also require that:

c) applicant states open their own quota-based "climate mobility" pathways allowing nationals of the most climate-vulnerable Pacific islands to settle on their shores.

A common travel area would demonstrate solidarity on two levels: Australia and New Zealand would be lifting barriers for citizens of the best-governed countries in the region, while the most resilient countries would be extending lifelines towards citizens of the most climate-vulnerable.

**WHY IT WILL WORK:** If history is any guide, change across the region will not first come from attempts at political and security assimilation, premised on the "strategic denial" of China's influence, but rather from horizontal integration: by removing barriers on the movement of data, capital and people.

The expansion of these "three freedoms", branching out from a nucleus of countries, has the potential to unite all Pacific island states in a common direction of travel, albeit at different speeds.

A digital single market and a common travel area for the Pacific would represent by far the most innovative forms of regional integration ever attempted, with the potential to boost national incomes through increased labour mobility and remittance flows, advance the region's collective response to climate change, and spur reforms that would strengthen government capacity and regional security.

Applying the logic of European integration to the Pacific island region is not the same as calling for a "Pacific EU". Australia is fortunate that a regional body and a Pacific-defined vision for a Blue Pacific Continent already exists to underpin these projects. It would be up to the member states collectively to decide the form of future political arrangements between them. It is conceivable that the grouping of island countries settles for a more decentralised union sustained principally by intergovernmental treaties, rather than bodies such as the European Commission.

Either way, the effects for Australia would be game-changing. Canberra would essentially acquire the EU's most powerful tool of foreign policy – its enlargement policy – for reshaping the dynamics of the region without the need to impose restrictions on the sovereignty of Pacific island countries.

The promise of two-way integration with a country representing more than 80 per cent of the PIF economy would make Pacific island governments more resistant to the risk of top-down elite capture. Opting out of these transformative regional ventures would raise the political stakes and narrow the choices available to any government wishing to play geopolitics at the expense of their people's future.

The greatest challenge to unlocking durable integration in the Pacific is not China but domestic political constraints in Australia. Its political class will need to forcefully convey to voters the strategic urgency and economic dividends of bringing the Pacific family together in unprecedented ways. As Brexit illustrated, projects of this nature rarely end well without the social licence to propel them forward. ■

## Reviews

***Divided Isles: Solomon Islands and the China Switch***
Edward Acton Cavanough
La Trobe University Press

Small Island Developing States (SIDS), many of which are in the Pacific region, have long struggled to overcome scepticism about their economic prospects. Indeed, policymakers have often deemed them unviable due to their narrow range of exports and heavy reliance on imports – a combination which is said to generate unparalleled levels of vulnerability to global market shocks. When you add their isolation and archipelagic geography, both of which increase supply chain costs, the unique development challenges for these island nations catalysed the growing SIDS agenda in international organisations. And that is before we even get to climate change.

Solomon Islands is distinctive because it is endowed with more natural resources – logging and mining – and a larger population than other SIDS in the Pacific region. It has also struggled to generate a tourism economy, which, along with financial services, has been the key to the economic success of most other SIDS, especially in the Caribbean. Indeed, the development paradox of most SIDS is that they are both highly vulnerable and relatively wealthy in GDP per capita terms. The development paradox of Solomon Islands, by contrast, is that increased resources, whether natural or granted in the form of aid and loans, never seem to make much of a difference to most ordinary citizens, especially those who live beyond the capital city, Honiara. As Edward Cavanough documents in *Divided Isles*, if you venture outside Honiara, you will find most villages do not have electricity or running water, and the cash economy primarily revolves around tiny shops that sell rice, canned fish and noodles.

Economic diversification has been the core postcolonial economic imperative of SIDS. One unconventional method of diversification is to sell sovereignty. Financial services and citizenship by investment schemes are common to the Caribbean. Pacific SIDS were late to this form of enclave capitalism and have had more success leasing access to territory. The parties to the Nauru Agreement – a fisheries agreement between eight Pacific states – sell access to their exclusive economic zones and by doing so control the largest sustainable tuna purse-seine fishery on earth. Palau, Federated States of Micronesia and Marshall Islands have entered into successive Compacts of Free Association with the United States, whose military is allowed freedom of movement through their territory and uses some islands as bases. Nauru and Papua New Guinea leased territory to Australia as asylum-seeker processing centres. These deals enabled the SIDS to increase their revenue streams, reduce their vulnerability and sustain a basic level of services.

Leasing territory has often been complemented by a range of other niche sovereignty sales, which might appear marginal to large states but have been important for the very smallest. Philately (stamp collecting) and numismatics (coin collecting), for example, have generated much needed foreign exchange in the past. The UK overseas territory of Anguilla is currently benefiting from a boom in sales of its internet domain name .ai, following the earlier success of Tuvalu, which capitalised on .tv. Fiji sends peacekeepers on UN missions. Marshall Islands, Cook Islands and Vanuatu are home to some of the world's largest shipping registries. SIDS have long traded their votes in international organisations. They have also traded in diplomatic recognition, especially switching between China and Taiwan. This latter form of sovereignty sale is the focus of *Divided Isles*.

In 2019, Prime Minister Manasseh Sogavare's government ended Solomon Islands' thirty-six-year relationship with Taiwan when it changed its recognition to China. The "switch" followed other recent moves by SIDS, including Kiribati, and was controversial, especially on Malaita, the most populous island in Solomon Islands. Malaita has played a pivotal role in the nation's politics, including during the period of civil unrest in the late 1990s and early 2000s commonly known as "the tensions". The premier of Malaita, Daniel Suidani, fronted a campaign that opposed the move. The subsequent political agitation threatened to wind back the peace that the Australian-led Regional Assistance Mission to Solomon Islands (RAMSI) had helped maintain between 2003 and 2017, at a cost of more than $2.5 billion. Australian troops returned to quell riots in November 2021. In 2022, Sogavare signed a security agreement with China to enable it to provide similar assistance. The move sent shockwaves around the region and thrust Solomon Islands into the consciousness of the Australian public during the 2022 Australian federal election campaign.

Cavanough provides the good oil on these events. The book is part journalistic exposé and part travelogue. At its best, it follows in a tradition of Australian journalism that provides a real-time account of key events in Pacific history, such as Mary-Louise O'Callaghan's or Sean Dorney's books on the Sandline affair. But it also contains elements of Paul Theroux's travel book *The Happy Isles of Oceania*, including an obligatory side trip to see the famous megapodes of Savo, or J. Maarten Troost's *The Sex Lives of Cannibals*. The mix of these genres creates a tension. Cavanough the journalist wants the reader to know that Solomon Islander politicians, and Sogavare in particular, are sophisticated strategists attempting to solve the country's economic problems by punching above their weight in world affairs. Cavanough the travel writer wants the reader to know he visited exotic places and met interesting and amusing characters. The problem is that while the travel writing is polished and adds excitement, humour and, probably, readers, it also dilutes the more sober journalistic message.

This matters because the book's main claim – that Australia should take Solomon Islands and Solomon Islanders more seriously – is an important one. In recent commentary, the country has often been viewed by outsiders as a domino toppled by China in its escalating geopolitical rivalry with the United States. Sogavare and Suidani have become much more famous than most Pacific politicians, with the former cast as a wannabe despot and the latter as a proverbial David standing up to a geopolitical Goliath. Cavanough the journalist wants us to know that on the ground, and particularly outside Honiara, things are much more complicated: COVID-19 hit SIDS economies especially hard; years of Australian intervention and aid have made little difference to the lives of ordinary citizens; basic services are in disarray or non-existent; inter-island politics shape political life in ways that only make sense to locals; and outsider policymakers continue to treat their counterparts with unwarranted contempt, apportioning blame for problems when it isn't always clear local politicians have the means to solve them. All these messages are significant enough that *Divided Isles* should be widely read.

What they amount to is a call for greater humility by international actors (see page 283 in particular). Cavanough shows the way in two crucial respects. First, he attempts to place the "switch" in a broader historical context, starting with the Spanish explorer Mendaña's visits to the islands in the mid-sixteenth century and continuing through British colonial rule and World War II. Some of the best passages are when his informants narrate this history from a Solomon Islands perspective. The point is that the story of the "switch" doesn't begin when Canberra discovered Solomon Islands in the early 2000s. And it won't end when the rivalry between China and the United States is resolved, one way or the other. That's because – and this is the second point about humility, made explicit by his inclusion of community perspectives – the core economic problem won't have gone away. In the current economic order, even the most successful SIDS must constantly search for new niches to ensure a basic way of life survives. Leveraging great-power rivalry is the diversification strategy that offers the greatest potential at this historical moment. The reminder Cavanough offers large states is: because the best the status quo offers is tiny shops with rice, canned fish and noodles, all Pacific SIDS should be giving this strategy a go.

*Jack Corbett*

---

DEFENCE

***The Echidna Strategy: Australia's Search for Power and Peace***
Sam Roggeveen
La Trobe University Press

Sam Roggeveen, director of the International Security Program at the Lowy Institute, has given us in *The Echidna Strategy: Australia's Search for Power and Peace* the clearest critique of AUKUS to date: a well-informed and systematic cross-examination of the foundational assumptions of our national security policy and force structure. Any serious analyst of these matters should read it.

Surprisingly, given his sweeping recommendations, the author declares himself a liberal conservative, in the tradition of Edmund Burke and Michael Oakeshott, not a "Beijing dove", an "anti-American" or a radical pacifist.

He recommends, nonetheless, radical adjustments to our foreign and defence policies. He believes that the world order and our strategic environment are changing so fundamentally that it is delusional to believe that AUKUS will ensure our security.

His argument proceeds from several clearly stated premises: that China will come to dominate Asia, that the United States will not find the will or the means to resist this development, and that we and other US allies will have to look after our own defence. This cannot be done, he thinks, by adopting an offensive posture towards China.

Based on these premises, he deduces that we ought to adopt a highly conservative, purely defensive military posture that does not threaten China, but would make Australia a hard target for any Chinese invasion or direct attack. Distance is Australia's single biggest defence asset, he asserts. "Beijing is closer to London than to Sydney" and China could, therefore, only ever deploy a small part of its military capabilities against us.

A combination of missiles, mines, cyber weapons, limited maritime denial capabilities and not much more air power than we currently have would suffice to deter or defeat such a deployment, Roggeveen believes. Our army need only be a constabulary and doesn't require tanks.

All this will strike many readers as attractive, sensible and well argued. But it is peppered with problems. For instance, a "constabulary" without such heavy armour would take grievous casualties if ordered to assault a dug-in enemy infantry. My 2007 report to the army on this subject spelt this out in detail.

As for distance, Tokyo is as far away as Beijing, yet the Japanese bombed Darwin and penetrated Sydney Harbour in early 1942. Only US naval and air power defeated Japan, with marginal input from us. And Beijing is not the likely theatre of operations. That would be the South China Sea, which is much closer – and through which a great deal of our vital maritime trade passes.

Instead of betting on the US alliance system in the 2020s – along with Tokyo and Seoul, Manila and Taipei – Roggeveen urges a closer strategic relationship with the long-neutralist and poorly armed Indonesia. Is this plausible? Cultivating Indonesia as our new great and powerful friend is a big, big call. It could not ever replace what the United States has long provided, even if it was willing to engage in a closer strategic relationship with Australia.

That Japan and South Korea may go nuclear if US extended deterrence was withdrawn doesn't appear to concern Roggeveen. He also declares that, in the new order he envisages, "liberal principles and human rights will have no place". That, surely, is a dystopian future. There are so many uncertainties and challenges entailed in going down such a path that one might have expected a professed conservative to recoil.

However, his argument is anchored in the belief that the United States is not threatened by the rise of China and therefore has insufficient incentive to seriously contest Xi's ambition to achieve primacy in Asia. If it does take China on and we join it, he argues, the odds are we will find ourselves on the losing side.

Moreover, he adds, if we acquire nuclear-powered submarines with Tomahawk missiles and launch attacks on Chinese territory with them, we will risk severe Chinese retaliation. If we escalate, he argues, we lose. Best, therefore, to abandon any capabilities that would even make it possible for us to escalate or threaten to do so.

We would, presumably, also close the US bases on our soil, starting with Pine Gap and Nurrungar, compromising US global operations well beyond our shores. He doesn't address this problem sufficiently. To keep the bases would make us a de facto US strategic asset and target in a war with China. However, to deter China, we need the US alliance and that means both keeping the US bases and doubling defence expenditure.

Roggeveen argues that all this would be far less expensive than AUKUS. If we went it alone, we would have to double or treble our defence expenditure, whereas, he argues, if we spend on defence and denial capabilities and give up long-range strike ambitions, we could actually *reduce* our expenditures while improving our survivability.

Arguing that we could do all this quite rapidly, he cites Germany's about-face after Russia invaded Ukraine on 24 February 2022, when, as he puts it, within four days Chancellor Olaf Scholz "overturned two decades of German foreign and defence policy", declared "implacable opposition" to Putin's war of aggression and announced a massive boost to German defence spending.

But Scholz, at least rhetorically, put Germany on the front foot. Roggeveen would put us on the back foot. He doesn't mention the decisions by Sweden and Finland to seek NATO membership in the wake of Putin's blatant aggression. Had they reaffirmed their neutrality, he might have used their behaviour as a model.

Perhaps we could move fast, but it's the direction that is in question. Japan and South Korea are working closely with the United States to buttress security understandings, while openly insisting on Taiwan's right to not be coerced by China.

To cast aside existing capabilities and allies as Roggeveen suggests would confuse our Quad dialogue partners, send a dubious message to Xi Jinping and require a radical rejigging of a post–Five Eyes intelligence and policy establishment. It's not clear that Roggeveen has quite thought through these very serious consequences of his strategy.

*Paul Monk*

# Correspondence

## "Usual Suspects" by Yun Jiang

### Albert Zhang

In the essay "Usual Suspects" (Australian Foreign Affairs 19), Yun Jiang highlights some of the dilemmas facing Chinese Australians as they find themselves caught between the Chinese Communist Party's (CCP) ethnonationalist policies and the spectre of systemic racism in Australia. In Jiang's view, Australia's focus on foreign interference from the People's Republic of China has been counterproductive and damaging for Chinese Australians.

As a fellow Australian of Chinese descent, I live with the ethnic and racial prejudices Jiang and others in the community experience. But rather than being disheartened by Australia's recent national security policies, I'm emboldened because Australia has become in many ways safer for Chinese Australians from Hong Kong, Xinjiang and Tibet, as well as those from the mainland, to participate in the public debate and be heard by the government. The fact that we are having this important conversation is one example that shows the public discourse maturing.

Jiang is right to claim that the Australian government's approach to foreign interference should be country-agnostic. However, the Australian government must prioritise investigations in proportion to the scale and potential harms of the threat. We shouldn't be surprised that Australia's limited resources are focused on countering interference by the Chinese government, which is the largest offender in this space. No other actor has the intent, personnel and resources to interfere in Australia's democracy at a scale like the CCP under Xi Jinping.

The Australian government doesn't focus solely on China, of course. The Minister for Home Affairs, Clare O'Neil, has publicly condemned transnational repression from Iran, and ASIO's director-general, Mike Burgess, has revealed that it dismantled a "hive" of spies who, according to media reports, were Russian intelligence officers.

Jiang claims that the Australian government's approach to assessing security risks relies on identifying "some nexus" or link to China's party-state. Australians should condemn any approach that assesses security risks solely based on loose associations with China, or anywhere else. After all, foreign interference is an act and, by the Australian government's definition, an activity that is "carried out by, or on behalf of, a foreign power, that is coercive, corrupting, deceptive or clandestine, and contrary to Australia's sovereignty, values and national interests".

In the case of international students from China, it isn't their pro-CCP views that are an issue but that Chinese diplomats set up and manage Chinese student associations and appoint their leaders, and that Chinese security officials directed student agents to infiltrate dissident groups and surveil other students. This has been reported on by Australian media and publicly confirmed by Chen Yonglin, a former Chinese diplomat who defected to Australia in 2005.

Likewise, the interference risks posed by Chinese technology companies, such as Tencent, ByteDance or Huawei, don't arise from their "Chineseness" but because the CCP, unlike the Australian or US governments, has the coercive power and legal authority granted by the National Intelligence Law to co-opt their platforms for collecting intelligence and manipulating the public opinion of other countries.

These risks are not speculative but have already happened. Early last year, the Canadian government detected an information operation on WeChat targeting Canadian politician Michael Chong, in which it assessed the CCP's role as highly probable. In 2018, multiple news reports confirmed that the African Union headquarters' internal servers in Addis Ababa, the bulk of which had been supplied by Huawei and paid for by the Chinese government, had been sending sensitive data to servers located in Shanghai every night for five years without the knowledge of the African Union. Zhang Yiming, the founder of ByteDance, has stated on the record that his products, such as TikTok, would serve the CCP's propaganda agenda.

Jiang claims that the national security community views the burdens placed on Chinese Australians as collateral damage to "ensure Australia is free from PRC influence". But it is Chinese Australians – including journalists, researchers and activists – who have led the debate and continue to call for the Australian government to do more to counter the CCP's interference.

I agree with Jiang that Australia's political leaders should do more to voice support for Chinese Australians' freedom of expression and right to participate in public debate. But it's an open question as to whether the government should be responsible for all the racist views of its citizens and media. The government has tried to be careful in distinguishing China's party-state from Chinese people, despite some abuses of language in the past. Jiang's argument could have been more compelling if she had offered more evidence that what she perceives as a rise in racial discrimination in Australia was primarily due to Australia's counter–foreign interference policies and not from organic, albeit misplaced, public reactions to the CCP's behaviour. We can see how sharply views of China under Xi's leadership have declined from polling by the Lowy Institute, which in 2023 revealed only 15 per cent of Australians trusted China to act responsibly in the world (in 2018 it was 52 per cent).

That is not to say everyone is absolved of responsibility. There have been numerous examples of sensational reporting of alleged foreign interference without strong evidence by a small but loud subsection of the media. These should not be seen as representative of Australia's overall approach to foreign interference and should be criticised, not to silence their voices but to improve the public debate and avoid further fuelling racist views.

Ultimately, I agree with one of Jiang's conclusions, that the Australian government should do more to explain the difference between benign and malign foreign influence. Too often, the government hasn't been forthcoming when explaining the threats to Australia, and how it is working to counter them.

But even with the lack of evidence presented by the government, all Australians can review the tomes of robust open-source research and high-quality investigative reporting that have shone sunlight on the CCP's interference in Australia. This work is important because it partly explains the government's national security decision-making and justifies Australia's concerns over the CCP's increasingly aggressive activities.

*Albert Zhang is an analyst with the Australian Strategic Policy Institute, specialising in cyber, technology and security.*

## Jieh-Yung Lo

Consider this: I was born in Melbourne; my parents came to Australia in 1978 as ethnic Chinese refugees from Vietnam; my father is a senior member and elder of the Chinese Australian community in Melbourne, where he co-founded both the Chao Feng Chinese Orchestra in 1982 (the first non-profit Chinese music orchestra registered in Australia) and *Han Sheng,* one of Australia's first Chinese-language current affairs magazines; I have known no country as my home other than Australia. Despite this, I was accused of committing treason against my country and our people simply because I expressed a moderate view of the People's Republic of China (PRC) and advocated for greater nuance in the public debate about the Australia–China bilateral relationship. In other words, this introduction – and the introductions of countless other Chinese Australians – features a different story to Yun Jiang's but echoes her concerns.

The nearly 1.4 million Australian residents identified as having Chinese ancestry and heritage make a significant contribution to the history and prosperity of this country. Like other multicultural communities, Chinese Australians face barriers to political and social participation, as well as to positions of influence and leadership, because of racism, discrimination, unconscious bias and, specifically, the existence of a "bamboo ceiling". I believe Chinese Australians experience particular complexities due to geopolitical tensions and to the way our policymakers have responded to foreign interference.

In 2017, in an opinion article in *The Sydney Morning Herald,* I was one of the first to use the term "collateral damage" to sum up the difficult circumstances we Chinese Australians have found ourselves in. Since then, the term has been widely employed by members of the Chinese Australian community reacting to what Jiang accurately describes as Australia's "singular focus on the PRC as the source of foreign interference". This public focus on foreign interference has put Chinese Australians in the spotlight in a way not seen since Federation. Whether we like it or not, we are being wedged in the middle of this debate because of our ethnicity and background. To make matters worse, Chinese Australians involved in the public debate have been forced to take a side, and the right side at that, to avoid condemnation – which is to denounce the CCP and, to an extent, the PRC.

Jiang is correct to point out that the public discourse on foreign influence and interference has had a significant impact on Australia's democracy and values. The Chinese Australian community has historically been one of this country's most vibrant and energetic. From cultural festivals to initiating people-to-people links between Australia and the PRC, and facilitating economic and business leads, Chinese Australians have always had a visible and active presence across our society and institutions. Since the increase in geopolitical tensions and the introduction of foreign interference laws, I have seen this vibrancy and activity dissipate. Many Chinese Australians now keep a low profile rather than seek public-facing roles or contribute to the Australia–China relationship. This is disappointing because, in today's rapidly shifting political and economic landscape, it is more crucial than ever for Chinese Australians to have their voices heard and amplified, and their leadership paths nurtured.

I recently coordinated and co-convened a program designed to empower Chinese Australians pursuing more visible leadership roles. Named after the first Australian barrister of Chinese and Asian heritage, the inaugural William Ah Ket Leadership Program – held in August 2023 – aimed to assist fifteen emerging Chinese Australian leaders in becoming more effective in their fields and, if relevant, in playing an active part in advancing Australia's relationship with the PRC. The four-day program, held by the Centre for Asian-Australian Leadership at the Australian National University – with support from the Australian government's National Foundation for Australia–China Relations – brought together academics, politicians, business leaders, commentators and leadership experts. In addition to establishing a vital network of peers, the program created a safe space for Chinese Australian professionals to discuss issues they are facing. A moment that has stayed with me was when a participant who had broken down in tears said a contentious relationship between Australia and the PRC had made it more difficult for her to take her children to visit their ancestral homeland in the PRC. She felt that the complications were further exacerbated by her Chinese Australian heritage and work in the Australian Public Service, a role she was not willing to give up due to the commitment and loyalty she has for Australia. Her reflections are just one example of the internal conflicts and challenges faced by many Chinese Australians – different stories that echo similar concerns.

The program's success shows that our multicultural heritage is indeed Australia's competitive edge, but it remains largely under-utilised and under-appreciated. If reactions from Jewish Australians, Palestinian Australians and Muslim Australians to recent events in Gaza have proven anything, it is that the wellbeing of Australia's multicultural communities is affected not only by geopolitics but by our foreign policy towards their country of origin or heritage. As such, the federal government needs to develop a foreign policy that places the voices of multicultural Australians at its centre.

I agree with Jiang that Chinese Australians play a vital role in business and investment, academia, research and cultural exchange, and are Australia's greatest asset in building a more successful relationship with the PRC. Policymakers and departments should consider consulting Chinese Australian leaders when making policies in order to support the community's needs and improve the bilateral relationship. A failure to engage Chinese Australians in the implementation of foreign interference legislation could undermine the country's social harmony, which is worth protecting at all costs. As Jiang correctly points out, "When combating foreign interference, social cohesion is an asset – it should not be seen as a distraction."

*Jieh-Yung Lo is the founding director of the Centre for Asian-Australian Leadership at the Australian National University.*

## Yun Jiang responds

The two pieces of correspondence offer a glimpse of the diverse opinions that exist in the Chinese Australian communities. Indeed, it would be a mistake to believe that all Chinese Australians share similar views on Australia's policy towards China, just like not all Indigenous people agreed on the Voice Referendum and not all Jewish people feel the same way about Israel.

I will address two issues arising from the correspondences: foreign interference from China compared to that from other countries, and the responsibility of the Australian government to address racism.

Albert Zhang believes that Australia should prioritise interference from the Chinese government because it is the biggest threat. I agree to an extent. It is possible that country-agnostic investigations would discover that the Chinese government is responsible for most interference activities, and therefore much of the resources are allocated to countering interference from China. This approach is not problematic.

What would be problematic is focusing investigations on threats from China while downplaying threats from elsewhere, because of the belief that it poses the biggest threat. This is akin to police focusing on crimes committed by one ethnic or racial group only.

We know that other countries engage in interference activities. Zhang listed two other countries: Iran and Russia. Notably, these two governments are already seen as malign pariahs by Australia. But even countries "friendly" to Australia can engage in interference.

The biggest story on foreign interference coming out of Canada last year was the assassination of a Sikh activist, Hardeep Singh Nijjar. Canada alleged that the Indian government was responsible, while India accused Canada of harbouring terrorists. The reaction in Australia to this blatant interference from India was much more muted than if China had done it. Does it mean that Australians care more about protecting the Chinese diaspora than the Sikh diaspora? No, this is simply because unlike China, Iran or Russia, India is seen as being on "our side", so any condemnations are moderated. As a result, Indian students expressing support for the Indian government's actions are usually not portrayed as suspicious or acting against Australia's interests. And Indian Australians are not being asked to choose between India and Australia.

Zhang is incorrect in asserting that "the CCP, unlike the Australian or US governments, has the coercive power and legal authority ... for collecting intelligence manipulating the public opinion of other countries". In fact, China's coercive power is much weaker and much less effective than the US's. Henry Farrell and Abraham Newman, in their book *Underground Empire: How America Weaponized the World Economy*, detailed the US government's coercive power, which it wields through its stranglehold on global finance, information and technology.

For example, the US government "demanded data on foreigners [from US technology companies], threatening harsh penalties for [those] that did not comply, while ordering them to keep their compliance secret". It seized data from companies such as Microsoft without any warrant. Furthermore, it claimed "jurisdiction over foreign banks that touched the US dollar and used its control of dollar clearing to discipline them". When the US sanctioned Carrie Lam, Hong Kong's then chief executive, even Chinese banks abided by the sanctions and did not provide her with a bank account.

Raising the actions of the United States does not mean condoning the actions of China. Of course, there are reasons that the Australian government or an individual might condemn interference activities of the Chinese government while turning a relative blind eye to those of others. As Natasha Kassam and Darren Lim wrote in a previous issue, "Hypocrisy and inconsistency are, and always will be, features of geopolitics. The powerful often claim to uphold certain values and standards, but regularly and rapidly discard these when their interests conflict."

Zhang has made an error that country or area specialists often do: believing that the country they study is exceptional, either exceptionally virtuous or exceptionally evil. And if you talk to people in the United States or China or India, many believe in their own versions of "exceptionalism". This is why comparing different countries is so important.

Zhang notes later that "it's an open question as to whether the government should be responsible for all the racist views of its citizens and media". I do not think policymakers can escape the responsibility to counter racism, and they should certainly not add to it. For example, some politicians may use dog-whistling to encourage racism and suspicions against Chinese Australians. As observed by Jieh-Yung Lo, they may promote the idea that it is reasonable to force Chinese Australians to take a side and to openly denounce the Chinese government. On the other hand, politicians could take racism seriously and proactively find ways to tackle all forms of it.

Lo suggests the federal government develop a foreign policy that places multicultural Australians at its centre. Under the current government, Australia's Indigenous heritage and multicultural identity are emphasised more than under the previous government. This is a good start. However, obstacles remain. The public service is currently not well equipped to integrate foreign policy with social policy such as multiculturalism.

The new emphasis on multiculturalism demonstrates that the government can choose different narratives to promote with regards to its foreign policy. So it would not be acceptable for a government to say increasing suspicions and discriminations are not its responsibility. I expect more from our government.

As a migrant, when I was younger, I did not see myself as a full Australian. I was grateful just to be here. I kept a low profile and avoided public debates. But now I ask myself: why should I or Lo or Zhang not expect the same rights and the same treatment as other Australians? We are just as Australian.

*Yun Jiang is the Australian Institute of International Affairs China Matters Fellow and a former policy adviser in the Australian government.*

---

# Back Issues

**ALL PRICES INCLUDE GST, $11.00 FLAT RATE POSTAGE AUSTRALIA WIDE.**

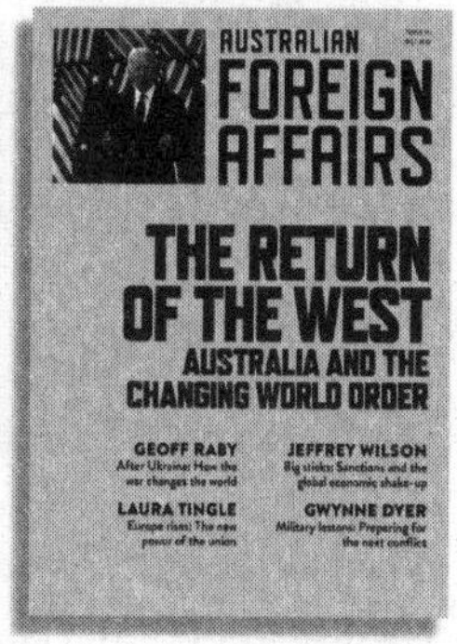


- ☐ **AFA3** ($19.99) Australia & Indonesia
- ☐ **AFA4** ($19.99) Defending Australia
- ☐ **AFA5** ($19.99) Are We Asian Yet?
- ☐ **AFA6** ($19.99) Our Sphere of Influence
- ☐ **AFA7** ($19.99) China Dependence
- ☐ **AFA8** ($19.99) Can We Trust America?
- ☐ **AFA9** ($19.99) Spy vs Spy
- ☐ **AFA10** ($19.99) Friends, Allies and Enemies
- ☐ **AFA11** ($19.99) The March of Autocracy
- ☐ **AFA12** ($19.99) Feeling the Heat
- ☐ **AFA13** ($19.99) India Rising?
- ☐ **AFA14** ($19.99) The Taiwan Choice
- ☐ **AFA15** ($22.99) Our Unstable Neighbourhood
- ☐ **AFA16** ($22.99) The Return of the West
- ☐ **AFA17** ($22.99) Girt by China
- ☐ **AFA18** ($22.99) We need to talk about America
- ☐ **AFA19** ($22.99) The New Domino Theory

**PAYMENT DETAILS** I enclose a cheque/money order made out to Schwartz Books Pty Ltd.
Or please debit my credit card (MasterCard, Visa or Amex accepted).

CARD NO. ☐☐☐☐☐☐☐☐☐☐☐☐☐☐☐☐

EXPIRY DATE / CCV AMOUNT $

CARDHOLDER'S NAME

SIGNATURE

NAME

ADDRESS

EMAIL PHONE

**Post or fax this form to:** Reply Paid 90094, Collingwood VIC 3066 **Freecall:** 1800 077 514 **or** +61 3 9486 0288
**Fax:** (03) 9011 6106 **Email:** subscribe@australianforeignaffairs.com **Website:** australianforeignaffairs.com
**Subscribe online at australianforeignaffairs.com/subscribe** (please do not send electronic scans of this form)

## The Back Page

FOREIGN POLICY CONCEPTS AND JARGON, EXPLAINED

# THE ALIGNMENT PROBLEM

**What is it:** The concern that artificial intelligence (AI) systems could pursue goals in ways that do not align with human values.

**Who coined it:** The term's use in AI has been credited to Stuart Russell (professor, UC Berkeley), who says AI systems are typically programmed with singular or instrumental goals and therefore behave differently to humans.

**Peak misalignment:** In 2003, philosopher Nick Bostrom (professor, Oxford) proposed one of the most famous AI alignment problems, in which a machine designed to make as many paperclips as possible turns human atoms into paperclips or destroys humanity to avoid being switched off. Other scenarios include machines that eliminate cancer by killing all humans or that make restaurant bookings by shutting down phone networks to prevent others making reservations.

**Alignment critics:** Some critics say AI is far from being able to unleash this paperclip-style destruction. Nir Eisikovits (professor, UMass Boston) has dismissed such scenarios as "science fiction", saying current technology lacks a capacity for "multilayer judgment" and does not have sufficient access to critical infrastructure to "start causing that kind of damage".

**The alignment solution:** Major AI firms – and all 193 United Nations member states – have backed initiatives to ensure that future research and technology lead to ethical outcomes. Last year, Stuart Russell claimed AI systems will be safer if they are built "so that they understand some things about what humans want, but they know there's a bunch of other stuff that they don't understand and they're uncertain about".